DON'T SCREW UP
HON. SEC.

The Omnidirectional Ramblings
of a Non-League Football Secretary

Stan Strickland

'You can fail at what you don't want, so you might as well take a chance on doing what you love.'

Jim Carrey

Introduction

I have decided having now retired from football admin to put down my thoughts of the twenty-five years I spent on and off as the secretary of a semi-pro football club. On more than one occasion I have given up the idea thinking am I going to be dragging up events that are best forgotten but then I have thought of all the wonderful memories and started up again. I will just have to see where it takes me.

I could always arrange to have it published posthumously to avoid any flak!

This will not be a match-by-match record it will be a personal account of my memories of events on and off the field with the intention of entertaining as well as informing.

It includes many, I hope, interesting anecdotes and one of the reasons I have included 'omnidirectional ramblings' in the sub-title of the book is that it will be just that with the right chronological order often suffering due to the passage of time and not always the greatest of considerations.

There is much to tell, I have been so lucky to be involved with two incredibly successful village football clubs.

I hope you enjoy, if not, I hope you keep it to yourself!

Stan Strickland
Isle of Anglesey
December 2020

'A SQUARE PEG IN A ROUND HOLE'

I was born in Liverpool on the second day of January 1943, at least I think I was, hardly a good start! My birth was registered at the city's Walton Hospital yet I have a vague memory of my mum telling me I was actually born in Southport. It could well have been true as many pregnant women were moved along the coast to give birth during World War II even though the last German air raid on Liverpool had taken place almost a year previously.

Southport born or not I consider myself a true Liverpudlian, I have never been particularly fond of the term Scouser.

Me, my mum Nora, my dad Bill, and my younger brother Brian lived at 116 Storrington Avenue in houses built for Royal Ordnance Factory workers. We were allocated a house because my dad worked in munitions at the ROF factory in Fazakerley, I can only imagine how dangerous his job was.

At the top of our road was the Norris Green Estate built in the 1930s although our road was a virtual cul-de-sac surrounded by green fields, an idyllic area for young kids to play. That all changed somewhat in the early 1950s when the Croxteth Estate was built at the bottom of our road. It meant we were now sandwiched between two of the biggest council house estates in Europe.

I was never quite sure what area we lived in, sometimes we said Croxteth, sometimes Norris Green or even Gillmoss though my mum often said West Derby as it sounded posher. Now there is a clear sign entering the road from the city end saying Croxteth, so I am from Croxteth.

Out two main interests as young kids were football and playing cowboys and indians. Both used up plenty of energy that left us pretty tired by the time we were called in. In fact we seemed to spend all our time outside playing.

My dad wasn't a great football enthusiast but I can recall him taking me to Goodison Park to watch Everton. We used to go high up in one of the double decker stands, it was such a thrill for a young lad. When I started going to the football on my own I was only allowed to go in the boy's pen at reserve games and by then I had chosen to watch Liverpool and when I got a little older and went to first team games on the Kop I was hooked for life.

I went to Broad Square Primary School in West Derby up until the age of eleven, it wasn't the nearest but mum and dad picked it out as a good school. They were right as I passed my eleven plus and then went to the Holt High School in Childwall. I was never that great at football, I've always talked a far better game, so never played for the school team although in later years I did go on to play for Old Holts.

Upon leaving school at sixteen with four GCE 'O' Levels I was taken on as an engineering apprentice by Lucas GTE Ltd part of the Joseph Lucas Group. They were situated in Bowring Park Road, Broadgreen, just across from where Ken Dodd lived in Thomas Lane! My dad worked there as a toolmaker and I always felt certain that influenced their decision to take me on. My dad was keen for me to get a trade as were many parents in those days.

Part way through my apprenticeship I was offered the opportunity to go and work in the laboratory at Girling across the Mersey in Bromborough, they made brakes and were also part of the Lucas Group. I jumped at the chance even though it meant I was never to complete my engineering apprenticeship a decision that I believe had a big influence on how my working career panned out over the coming years.

The travel each day eventually became a pain, a bus then the train or ferry across the river then another bus so when I saw a job advertised in 1966 for a laboratory assistant at AC Delco in Kirkby I applied. An American company, part of General Motors, the salary was far better and of course travel was considerably less. Anyway I got the job despite competition from the big boss's son.

I moved out of Storrington Avenue at the end of 1969 when I married Sally Greenwood from Stockport. We moved into a ground floor flat on Queens Drive in Walton, within easy reach of both football grounds as it happened! We lived there for about twelve months before buying a brand new semi-detached dormer bungalow in Ledger Road, Haydock after Sally became pregnant with our first child, Paul. Then our two daughters came along, Kerrie and Jennie.

Our home at Haydock, most famous for the racecourse, had open views at the back but over the years we lost that as more and more houses were built until we felt we were living at the centre of a large estate. We opted to move on.

About 1980 we bought a three bedroomed semi in Ormskirk a market town midway between Liverpool and Preston. The house at 109 Redgate had glorious views over open farmland at the rear and was only a ten minute walk from the town centre.

As well as being a regular supporter of Liverpool over the years going to most home games and many away I also took an interest in the non-league scene and had visited most of the local grounds at some time including South Liverpool, New Brighton, Marine, Burscough, Skelmersdale United and Guinness Exports.

Now settled in Ormskirk an unexpected opportunity for change arose late in 1992. I was 49 at the time, approaching my fiftieth, when an offer was made by General Motors of a voluntary redundancy package consisting of a lump sum and a monthly pension. By then I had 26 years service so the terms seemed attractive although the idea of 'retiring' at 50 seemed faintly ridiculous.

At AC Delco, second left. Visit of American GM boss

Sally knew that I was not really happy in my work. To be honest I always felt a little like a square peg in a round hole working as an engineer in a company making car components. After my period as a laboratory assistant, or the more impressive sounding analytical chemist as I was occasionally described, I had been pushed back into product engineering where the effects of my truncated apprenticeship came back to haunt me. I had missed out on much of my training.

Even when I had started my apprenticeship I felt disadvantaged having had more of an academic education in a grammar school while much of the intake had been to technical college and were already familiar with the basics of engineering, both theoretical and practical.

Additional to all that I had very little interest in cars except as a means of transport, not ideal for someone employed by General Motors.

Encouraged and supported by the wonderful Sally I applied to take the package on offer not having a clue what I would do if accepted. Before the end of 1992 I got word that I had been successful and I would leave the company in March 1993.

In many ways it was a turning point in my life.

'NEW FOUND FREEDOM'

General Motors had been a great company, I was paid well, I was never out of work and I enjoyed the crack with my workmates yet I felt a great sense of relief to leave although I would hate anyone to think I was unappreciative of the part they played in providing for our family especially through those years when the kids were young.

I would like to think I gave them value for money though to be honest I am never at my best if I am not passionate and enthusiastic about a subject and I never really offered GM that.

My years of regularly attending Liverpool games had pretty well ended through choice when we had children although I still remained a passionate supporter. Living in Ormskirk the nearest football club was up the A59 at Burscough where I occasionally attended games at Victoria Park although not yet what you would call a supporter. In fact I had probably been to local rivals Skelmersdale United's ground just as many times.

As soon as I knew I would be leaving I started to think about how I could best take advantage of this new found freedom. I felt a need to get into something I could really get passionate about and when I saw an advert in a Burscough programme for a vacancy for secretary I applied even though I knew it was not a paid position.

I had already got to know Mark Parr quite well through a mutual interest in selling football programmes. Mark was the son of Burscough chairman Frank Parr and whether he put in a word for me I have no idea but after meeting Frank I was offered the job.

So while I was still working out my final weeks as a GM employee I began as the new secretary of Burscough Football Club.

The guy assigned to show me the ropes was previous secretary Mike Woods. Mike was also the treasurer and right away I sensed some tension in the air. It soon became clear that Mike's preference was to give up the treasurer's job and continue as secretary! I thought, I'll leave that one with the chairman, I had zero interest in being treasurer.

Anyway Frank made it clear I was now secretary and to be fair to Mike he gave me a great deal of help during those early days as I was finding my feet. Secretary is a very responsible position with plenty of pitfalls that can end up costing the club money and, the biggest sin of all, costing the team points or a place in a cup competition if you get things wrong. Hence the title of this book: 'Don't Screw Up Hon. Sec.'

Although it is a long time ago now I reckon my first game acting as secretary was away to Blackpool Mechanics on Saturday 19th December 1992 with Mike Woods there to guide me. I remember being intrigued that there were three Football stadiums virtually in a row; Mechanics, Blackpool Wren Rovers and Squires Gate.

My main job on match days was to collect the team from the manager, make absolutely certain it was filled in correctly on the team sheet and present it alongside the opposition secretary to the referee normally no later than thirty minutes before kick-off. I learned early on to tell managers not to use player's nicknames on the list they gave me, a potential cause of mistakes.

To a certain extent once that was done I could then relax and enjoy the game something I have always carried through as a must during my many years as a secretary, never forgetting it is ultimately about the football on the pitch.

Known as the Linnets and with a proud history Burscough at that time were playing in the First Division of the North West Counties Football League having been promoted from Division Two.

I soon realised that I needed to be on a quick learning curve with such a great deal of experience already at the club. People like vice-chairman Stuart Heaps, future president Rod Cottam and committee man Roy Baldwin had been at the club for years while I was a complete novice. Most of all chairman Frank Parr had joined the club committee as an 18 year old back in 1946 when the club was founded and was already something of a club legend and closing in on 50 years service.

Frank was a very strong personality who like many northern football club chairmen could be quite brusque in manner at times. Mike had warned me that Frank had a tendency to take over arrangements when a big game came along. While remaining respectful I was determined that having taken on the role I would carry out my secretarial duties in the way I felt right. I could also be quite strong minded. It would be tested on both sides over the years that followed!

The manager when I joined was Russ Perkins. You could not meet a nicer man than Russ and it didn't take me long to appreciate he was a firm believer in playing entertaining, attacking football. He was a joy to work with, always so polite and appreciative. I called at Russ's house in Birkdale one time for some reason, he lived just across the road from Kenny Dalglish, and received such a warm welcome from him and his wife.

Those first few months at Burscough were an education to witness both the professional way the club was run off the field and the quality of the football on it. I particularly remember the experienced Tony Quinn in midfield, young striker Gary Martindale and the skilful Kevin Still from that team. Kevin was something of an enigma as he never really fully committed to football having other interests and far too soon drifted away from the game. He was one of the best players I saw play for Burscough. Gary was the first player I signed as secretary! Russ had brought him from Liverpool side St Dominics. He will go on to feature quite prominently in my story in a way we could never have imagined, not in our wildest dreams.

I was in my element working in football after the inevitable tensions of being employed in an American owned factory where production targets were always a highly demanding priority. I was very mindful, however, that it wasn't a proper job bringing money into our family something I knew I would have to get around to discussing with Sally who was continuing to work at the local hospital in Ormskirk.

Before leaving GM Sally and I had several meetings with professional financial advisers on how best to invest the lump sum we would receive. I was not greatly impressed and in the end decided to choose and manage the investments myself, one of the best decisions I ever made.

In early March a two-legged victory over Prescot took Burscough through to the League Cup Final where they would face Nantwich Town at Gigg Lane, Bury. It was proving quite a baptism for me as a newcomer to the club when later in the month another big game appeared on the horizon.

In the semi-final of the Liverpool Senior Cup we were drawn away to Everton. It had been traditional that the venue for these games against Liverpool and Everton were switched to the ground of the non-league club with the possibility of a large crowd and a lucrative pay day for their smaller brethren.

On this occasion, however, Everton manager Howard Kendall decided he wanted the game played at Goodison Park. I think it's true to say that despite the loss of potential income we were all delighted, certainly I was. Opportunities to play at Goodison or Anfield had become increasingly scarce as the senior clubs became more protective of their pitches.

Whatever impression I had made on Frank during my few weeks as secretary I don't recall any interference as the big game at Goodison loomed. I like to think he was confident in my ability by then.

So three months after becoming secretary of Burscough Football Club here I was sat in the director's box at Goodison Park having completed the match arrangements with the Everton secretary. The home side included David Unsworth and Scottish international Maurice 'Mo' Johnson in their line-up and enjoyed the greater share of possession though it didn't stop us deservedly going on to win 2-0 with first half goals from our two full backs, Brendan Doyle and Andy Doyle.

Young Ian Owen had been outstanding in central defence as Everton mounted increasing pressure after the interval in search of a goal that never came. The Liverpool Daily Post reported: 'Brilliant Burscough dump their more illustrious opponents out of Liverpool Senior Cup'.

It wasn't all serious stuff. During one game at Burscough that season there was some light 'relief' as during a lengthy stoppage for an injury Burscough keeper Alan Robinson decided to hop over the wall and go for a pee in the gent's urinal at the Mart Lane end. He reappeared a few moments later and took up his position back in goal. Just as the ref was getting ready to restart the game his attention was attracted by the waving flag of a linesman who had witnessed the evil deed and 'Robbo' was booked for leaving the field without permission I guess though I preferred to believe it was cos he didn't wash his hands!

My first season with the club was to end with two cup finals!

With manager Russ Perkins on holiday in America we faced Nantwich Town in the League Cup final on Friday 22nd April 1993. We had lost the same final at the same venue the previous year but this time there was to be no disappointment as goals from Brendan Doyle and Sean Togher put us two goals ahead and although the Cheshire side pulled a goal back it was Burscough skipper Tony Quinn who walked up the steps to lift the magnificent trophy.

It was Tuesday 11th May before we got around to playing Southport in the Liverpool Senior Cup Final, the venue again Goodison Park. The crowd of 2,000 might have been dwarfed by the size of the stadium though it didn't prevent a good atmosphere between the rival fans. Having just won promotion to the Conference Southport were strong favourites and came out winners 2-1 but not before we had outplayed them for long periods of the game. Kevin Still was the Burscough scorer in what was the club's 68th game of the season.

The club finished the league season in tenth place, not bad for a first season back in the top division, although more of a worry was the 68 goals conceded, only two clubs having finished with a worse defensive record.

'IT IS A F**KING FOOTBALL PITCH BILL'

I had got to know the people around the club during those first few months and begun to appreciate how well they worked as a team. Frank certainly led the way. He let me know in no uncertain terms early on that 'we set our own standards at Burscough' after I suggested following the example of another club. He was right of course. Perhaps Frank's most valuable characteristic was his stickability. No matter how bad anything got and finance was always a problem there was never any chance of him walking away.

Rod Cottam was club physio at the time and the main link between the committee and the manager. Rod went on to be president and all these years later is still the president and has remained loyal to the club through so much upheaval. It is not widely known outside the club but there is many a player we would not have been able to sign only for a 'quiet word' from Rod. I've never asked what was said or what was offered but I know it to be true. In many ways Rod could be considered a peacemaker! Tensions could run quite high particularly on match days, I know, I could often be the worst offender.

Stuart Heaps was the vice-chairman and is another still involved with the club. Stuart worked in that most thankless of areas, fundraising. He managed the club lottery and was usually in charge of boardroom hospitality. As the club had long sold its social club gate money, sponsorship and the lottery were the club's main source of income. Very few people have given as much to the club as Stuart.

Bill Fairclough was our groundsman and so proud of 'his' pitch. He used to watch like a hawk during games and training to ensure nobody took liberties. Even linesmen felt his wrath if they ran on the line rather than just behind it. I had many 'discussions' with Bill about games going ahead particularly reserve and youth games where the club rather than a referee usually decided. I remember one 'discussion' ending with me losing my rag and shouting at him: 'It is a fucking FOOTBALL pitch Bill!' Whatever, Bill cared passionately about the club and we lost him far too soon.

Sylvia and Gordon Cottle from Ormskirk were a big part of the club at that time always ready to canvass for new lottery members. Sylvia also used to run the canteen on match days in the wooden refreshment hut alongside the stand. Gordon did a tremendous amount in the community promoting the club amongst young people in particular. They left the club under a cloud several years later and I blame myself for that, they were a big loss to the club. I hope to be brave enough to admit to my mistakes in this book, of which there were many. Having said that I don't intend to be too immodest about any sense of achievement I feel!

Mark Parr was the chairman's son who had inherited his father's get up and go. He had an office close to the ground in Martland Mill where he initially ran a football programme catalogue and sold enamel badges before eventually expanding the business into many sports and promotional related products. He printed the matchday programme and was heavily involved in sponsorship, advertising and promotions. He organised many of the one-off fundraising evenings. I was to work closely with Mark over many years.

Roy Baldwin was on the club committee at that time and would remain so during the whole time I was at the club. He had served many years with Frank. Roy was one that did many of those not so glamorous tasks around a club that don't always get the appreciation they deserve. At least that's how I feel looking back. He was very knowledgeable about football and I learned a very good cricketer. Roy had a speech impediment and although it never seemed to bother him it did mean occasionally having to ask him to repeat what he said which I never liked doing. It was only when I travelled across from Anglesey to his funeral in May 2013 that I learned what a full life he had experienced.

By now I was feeling one of the lads and getting more confident by the day. I have always had strong ideas about how a football club should develop and over the coming years I like to think I played a part in bringing some of those ideas into practice. But I am getting ahead of myself.

Superstition can often be prevalent in football. At that time the secretary's office was situated under and towards the back of the main stand. There was a toilet that was accessed from the office and on occasions Russ would come into the office, ask to borrow a programme then go for a crap. After a while we began to joke that we always seemed to win when Russ went through this pre-match ritual. From then on we were always on tenterhooks waiting to see if he appeared!

All my passion for what I was doing had returned and I think Sally was aware of a much happier husband and was content to let me go with the flow, as they say. One advantage I guess was that I was so occupied I wasn't getting under her feet in my 'retirement'. Perhaps if we had been struggling to put food on the table she might have taken a different view.

It was no surprise, I was so much in my element. Football had always been my big love, supporting Liverpool being a passion most of my life then around 1979 I ran a team for three years in the Skelmersdale Sunday League and after that refereed in that league and the Ormskirk Sunday League for three years. Nothing on the scale of Burscough of course but all good experience nevertheless.

'FOOTBALL THAT HAD ME DROOLING'

Being my first close season it was quite intimidating yet it was soon to be one of my favourite times of the year with the excitement of new signings and the possibility of large crowds for attractive pre-season games against senior opposition and the chance of a few bob in the bank plus the anticipation of the release of league fixtures and cup draws.

It is a time when everyone is optimistic with a fresh start ahead, the pitch and ground are looking immaculate after a hard working summer of preparation and with a bit of luck the sun is shining as well, what's not to like? I used to love going down to the ground during the week, shutting the gate and taking in the silence at Victoria Park. Although close to the village centre it was like being in the country and I would often sit quietly at the back of the stand for a while enjoying looking out over the open farmland towards Crabtree and Southport before doing a bit of filing or something in the office.

One of my early learning experiences had been to make myself familiar with all the paperwork involved in registering players, applying for international clearance, entering various competitions, renewing player insurance, etc as well as making myself familiar with rulebooks for various league and cup competitions.

Most of our players were registered on non-contract terms. A player would normally only be offered a contract if it was felt he might attract the attention of a bigger club and a possible transfer fee. We became particularly good at that.

Mike Woods had finished as treasurer at the end of 1992-93 season and Frank brought in Peter Nelson in his place. Peter had accounting qualifications as I recall. He was a

Yorkshireman who had previous experience with Bradford Park Avenue FC. His son Roger also became involved with the club helping out with admission at the turnstiles.

Dave Whittle joined the committee. Dave was a bank manager but was never afraid to get his hands dirty, often to be seen sweeping or mopping out the changing rooms after a game. His son Stuart was a player with the club as was Russ's son Steve. Steve Perkins never really fully won over the regulars at Victoria Park although he gained the last laugh as he went on to become a full-time professional at Plymouth Argyle and play for England at semi-professional level.

If my first season had been eventful for two visits to Goodison Park and the winning of a cup final then my second season was to prove no less eventful although for different reasons!

It was to be a season when I witnessed football that had me drooling. Russ's brand of football led to goals galore. Twenty seven years later I can still vividly recall standing on the touchline away to Maine Road in Manchester thinking I have never seen non-league football played as good as this anywhere. It was majestic as we stroked the ball around with superb aplomb, winning 6-1 in the third game of the season. Gary Martindale got a hat-trick in what was the start of a prolific strike partnership with newly signed Mick McDonough. I seem to recall Gary's brother Colin played in that game.

Mick was a great young lad but always looked older than he was due to thinning hair. He also used to occasionally suffer from gout, that didn't do his street cred a lot of good either! I just hope he never reads this!

Midfielder Alex Russell had taken a couple of steps down to join us from Morecambe. It was almost certainly the best decision he ever made in football. More on that later.

This is a book about my experiences during 25 years in semi-pro football so it is not intended to be a match-by-match account. Suffice to say during 1993-94 season Burscough scored an incredible 107 league goals yet only finished third, a big improvement on last season's tenth however. Atherton LR had won the league for the second successive year, this time being promoted.

One memorable home game in February saw us beat Glossop 8-0. What a team we then had. New signing Kevin Formby, a local Ormskirk lad who had also stepped down a level, got a hat-trick and with Martindale, Kevin Still and the pony tailed Tommy Knox, a real crowd favourite, also amongst the scorers it was little wonder that we at times destroyed the opposition. Later that month our fixture away to Clitheroe ended with a 5-0 win, Martindale scoring four with one coming from a thundering low shot from so far out we were on the pitch at the finish estimating the distance. We reckoned a good forty yards! The vagaries of football could not have been better illustrated when three weeks after thrashing Glossop we lost by three goals to nil at their place!

Radio Lancashire had a Friday night non-league show and I was asked to go along to their studios in Blackburn to participate one week. A regular contributor was Ian McGarry who was then Darwen manager and quite a character. I could tell Ian had a soft spot for Burscough and Russ and he said quite early on in the discussion that we were the best side in the top division. I agreed and hoping we were outside the Atherton listening area added Atherton LR had a less expansive style of play that might be boring to some yet was proving successful. I enjoyed being part of the broadcast.

The truth was in football terms we were by far the best team in the league. We actually scored 24 more goals than champions Atherton LR.

Later in the season Russ spoke in glowing terms about Gary Martindale to the Liverpool Echo who by then was up around the 30 goal mark. Apparently the article alerted Bolton Wanderers manager Bruce Rioch which was to trigger of a quite incredible chain of events.

A presentation from West Lancashire District Council

Thursday 24th March 1994 was transfer deadline day and for me a new and exciting experience as following a trial game with Bolton the Burnden Park club came in with an offer for Martindale that was accepted by the club. The transfer fee was £10,000 with a sell-on clause.

Even more exciting for me later in the day Rochdale came in with an offer for Kevin Formby. There was one major problem, Kevin was not on contract. After some discussion Kevin agreed to sign a contract so the transfer could go ahead and Burscough would get a transfer fee. I ended up meeting him with the contract outside Mahood's sports shop in Ormskirk where he worked.

There was then frantic activity to get the paperwork sorted

before the 5pm deadline. I can remember being in Mark Parr's office high up in Martland Mill and getting the forms faxed through to the FA with only minutes to spare. The fee for Kevin Formby as I recall eventually reached £11,000.

Verdi Godwin was a big influence around the club at that time although his name might not have been widely known to supporters. He was regularly in attendance as a scout at Burscough home games and had an excellent eye for talent. Verdi had a long career as a player in professional football, Blackburn Rovers and Stoke City being two of his clubs. He also played for Tranmere Rovers in the fifties and I feel certain I saw him play when my Uncle Harry used to take me to games at Prenton Park as a kid. He had been a lifeguard on Southport beach for 36 years, being awarded the British Empire Medal for his services.

He was a great friend of Dave Hughes, who will feature shortly, and had some excellent contacts in the game, one being Rochdale manager Dave Sutton. We can feel sure Verdi had a big hand in Kevin Formby's transfer then, at the season's end, the transfer of Alex Russell also to Rochdale. I remember the transfer fee we received for Alex to be £9,000 which meant a total of £30,000 coming into the club's coffers, no wonder Frank effused about it being 'the proudest time in the 48 years I have been associated with the club.'

I always took a great interest in the career of players that had left the club to join the higher ranks. There was a feeling of real pride.

Gary Martindale never made the first team at Bolton and was released on a free so our sell-on amounted to nothing. He then signed for Peterborough United who later sold him to Notts County for £175,000. More in hope than expectation I sent a letter to Peterborough telling them how we had missed out on the sell-on and asking if they would consider a donation. In fairness they replied but it was such a tale of woe about their finances that I almost sent them a fiver! Gary went on to score a sensational goal for County in the 1996 Division Two play-off semi-final to take them to Wembley.

Kevin Formby went on to play for Rochdale against Liverpool at Anfield in the 1995-96 FA Cup. He also had the experience of playing at Wembley for Southport two years later in an FA Trophy Final.

Alex Russell perhaps more than any forged a long and distinguished career in the Football League with clubs including Rochdale, Cambridge United, Torquay United and Bristol City. Alex proved particularly astute in the way he managed his career no doubt with guidance from his dad, also Alex, who had been a professional himself.

In April we got a phone call from Preston North End assistant manager Gary Peters asking if they could train on Victoria Park. At the time they had their infamous plastic pitch and were due to go to Chester the following weekend so they wanted to hold a training session on a decent grass surface. Frank began to haggle about a price and I quickly realised this was just going to irritate them, they were a big local club who could do us some favours. I got on the phone and told Gary they would be welcome to use the pitch with no charge. It was perhaps the first time I stood up to Frank in such a direct way. I was right though, the following August they sent virtually a first team for a pre-season game and we got a crowd of about 800 with gate receipts to match and they never asked for a penny. They went on to visit us regularly pre-season, I can even recall David Moyes bringing a team eight years later!

The same month we played an away game at Blackpool Wren Rovers that I remember most for being served refreshments in the boardroom by two of the Nolan Sisters. One was the eldest sister Anne Nolan who was married to Rovers' manager Brian

Wilson. We won 1-0 so we were all in the mood for dancing!! Sorry.

We had no trophies to show at the season's end but, by God, Russ and the players had given us some fabulous entertainment the penultimate home game ending in a quite incredible 9-3 win at home to Nantwich Town, Russell getting four and no doubt sealing that transfer into the Football League. Perhaps the season was best summed up as we lost our final home game to Atherton LR......1-0!!!

I was now well settled at the club and enjoying every minute, gradually spreading my wings a little including contributing to the matchday programme and also more and more liaising with the press, specifically Geoff Howard the sports editor at the Ormskirk Advertiser.

At this time the club had a youth team that was doing very well managed by Barry Beesley and Kevin Downey. I recall some of the players; Michael Stokes, Michael Finch, Trevor Spencer, Ryan Bowen and Steve Perkins, mostly fairly local lads. Before I had arrived the team had faced Preston North End in the FA Youth Cup that season.

The youth team was of great interest to me, I was strongly of the opinion we should do everything possible to attract the best young players to the club by spreading our net if necessary, not only as potential first teamers but also to raise the profile of the club. The FA Youth Cup is a highly prestigious national competition.

'TREMENDOUS SPONSORSHIP DEAL'

For the duration of the time I had been at Burscough the club's main sponsor had been Bluelline Taxis of Ormskirk. I asked how much they paid per season and was told £500.

There was a company on the local industrial estate making a lot of noise nationally selling computers mail order. I actually bought some equipment from them myself, they were called Crown Computer Products. With nothing to lose I wrote a letter to their CEO Malcolm Jamieson telling him a little about the club with particular emphasise on the club's potential like a possible Wembley appearance. I got a reply asking me to go in and see him. He was obviously very interested, he told me he had been considering sponsoring Tranmere Rovers. He asked me what was the cost of sponsorship and I quoted him £5,000 per season. He never blinked and although there was much work still to be done we effectively struck a deal there and then. He did request that the £5,000 be paid in instalments over the season and that was agreed as well.

We were now dealing with a far larger company than Bluelline with a far bigger profile and expectations to match. Everything had to be spot on, their logo on the shirts and on the programme, specific Pantone colours of the logo had to adhered to and they wanted a redesign of the rather tired looking club badge. I ended up working with one of Crown's graphic designers to achieve that and in my view it was a big improvement. We also had a big splash in the local papers including the Liverpool Echo.

I felt I was now contributing something to the club, it was a tremendous sponsorship deal.

Contributing yes but one of my 'bright' ideas was to suggest that the winners of the club's Cashline Lottery would get free entry into the National Lottery meaning we could use the slogan 'become a millionaire with Burscough's Cashline Lottery.' It sounded great in theory though I don't think it generated many more new members and likely created more work for Stuart.

Another far better idea I had was to set up a Club Information Line. It was on the club's landline phone so not a premium rate call. I had found that I could access the answerphone remotely with my mobile using a PIN number and give details of fixtures, postponements, cup draws, results and scorers, etc, particularly useful if we were playing away. It proved very popular.

Having finished a creditable third it is a fact of life that a manager is then under pressure to improve still further. Whether we were ready or not for promotion to the Northern Premier League was another matter but the target was set high for Russ.

Work had been going on around the ground in preparation for possible promotion. A covered terraced stand with a capacity of 500 had been erected on the Barons side, tip-up seating had replaced the bench seating in the main stand. I recall drawing out the seating plan for the stand and John Moorcroft fitting them. Additional rooms had also been created under the stand including a new office I shared with the treasurer (away from any toilets!) and the changing rooms had been increased in size. Victoria Park had become a really impressive stadium.

I asked for the new office to have a stable door fitted and it was done. It meant that people didn't have to physically enter the office anymore. Previously it could be like Lime Street Station at times. I was always a bit tense pre-match until the team sheet had been safely deposited with the ref. It is a period when a lack of concentration can lead to a costly mistake.

It was to be the national cup competitions that would attract the headlines in 1994-95 season. Drawn at home to Congleton Town in the second qualifying round of the FA Cup the sides could not be separated after three attempts leading to a fourth game at Congleton and talk of cup replay records being set. The winners were due to play Morecambe and with time running out and Burscough leading I was already planning my phone call to the Shrimp's secretary Neil Marsdin confirming our game with them. Unfortunately it all then fell apart and we ended heavily beaten in extra-time.

'FEEL AN ABSOLUTE JERK'

The FA Vase was the competition we felt we could win and the prospect of a Wembley final was always the glamorous prize on the horizon. The truth was that if we got promoted we would no longer be eligible to enter the Vase we would have to enter the FA Trophy instead and with all the Conference clubs included it was a competition in which we would never stand an earthly.

There is one game I still recall from that season. We were due to play at Glossop in December and Russ was really stuck for a striker. Through his contacts he arranged to take a player on loan from Altrincham. The player's name was Lee Ramoon. He was from the Cayman Islands and in the UK studying at university. He was living in student digs in Altrincham.

I digress slightly here. During all the time I was at Burscough the only expenses I ever claimed were for things like stamps, envelopes, printer cartridges and paper, etc, items that were very much part of being secretary. I cannot recall me ever claiming for petrol for example and, by God, did I cover some miles!

I say this because if the manager wanted to sign a player I was pretty well available day or night because I knew it was for the benefit of the team so off I set midweek to Altrincham where I got Lee to sign the necessary forms. He met us at the Glossop ground the following Saturday. The mist was swirling around the chimney of a nearby mill high up in the Peak District as we kicked off, it must have seemed a million miles from the tropical beaches of his homeland. Lee started well but seemed to fade as the combination of the weather and the close attention of a couple of local mountain men in defence took their toll. He was a nice lad I recall having a pint with him after the game. Lee played just that once for

Burscough and to this day likely has no idea where it is.

I was reminded of our connection with Lee many years later. He first played for the Cayman Islands national team at 14 and went on to play for them more than 200 times often as captain. In 2004 Lee was awarded the FIFA Order of Merit, it is the highest honour awarded by FIFA. Described as a role model for young people in his country he travelled to Paris to receive the award from George Weah. I sent an email congratulating him and he wrote back that he still remembered that game for Burscough.

Stan Harvey had come on board the club committee and what a great addition Stan proved to be. Only small and in his seventies he was quite probably the fittest of us all. Stan fussed about everything, I often used to say to him he would make someone a wonderful wife, but he was a grafter and just got on with things and helped make Victoria Park look better than ever. By this time I was doing much of the programme although Mark and I were listed as joint editors. Stan was one who made the effort worthwhile as he read it from cover to cover always ready to point out any errors. He particularly liked a club focus page I did about tittle tattle and gossipy things around the club.

Stan was always to be found busy under the stand or around the ground. I recall one time him being in the roof space above the away changing room and falling through the ceiling. He just bounced!

I was sat in the stand at one game, I think against Chadderton, when the ball went high over the wall into Mart Lane followed by the sound of breaking glass. Of course everyone cheered including me before I thought on my car was parked thereabouts. Sure enough it had gone straight through my back window. Funny thing was Mrs Baldwin from the house opposite the ground had swept all the glass up put it in a box and left it in the back of my car. Bless her, but I couldn't help joking to others did she mean me to stick it back together? When the Autoglass man came he said park front side facing as it is toughened glass, obvious I guess but advice I have carried with me until this very day.

I always liked to have a look out for players of talent, I think that's what those of us sometimes described as non-football people often did. The ground was hired out privately one night to Reebok for a game when I saw two players who really impressed. I spoke to them in the Barons after the game and got their names and phone numbers, Peter Crane and John Toner. I told Russ and he did contact Crane who signed for us and played a couple of games. I don't know if he talked to seventeen year old Toner who went on to play ten years full-time with TNS in the Welsh Premier League and remains one of the all-time record goal scorers in Welsh football.

We began the FA Vase in the second round due to our previous good record in the competition and after beating Brigg Town at home we were drawn away to Arnold Town meaning a long trip down to Nottinghamshire. My main memory of this game is of dancing like a dervish with Gordon Cottle when a late goal from Mike Fagan gave us victory by three goals to two. Mike was the son of Liverpool legend Joe Fagan.

Brandon United were to be our next opponents, an unknown quantity from the Northern League. Burscough resident and former England international Bob Langton was our invited Guest of Honour that day. The game at Victoria Park led to a comfortable 3-0 win with John Brady, Kevin Still and Robbie Cowley our scorers. John Brady had rejoined the club having been part of the Burscough side that won the inaugural North West Counties League Division Championship back in 1982-83 season while Robbie Cowley was a fearsome striker.

Although Robbie carried one or two extra pounds his speed over ten yards was lethal giving him the advantage over his marker. I have great memories of the way Robbie put the ball away, he went on to get 30 goals that season.

Keith Crawford remembers a game at Great Harwood overhearing their manager telling his players: 'Look out for Cowley, he's eaten all the pies but scores goals for fun.' We won 5-2 and Robbie got three. Keith also reckons Robbie got 50 plus goals one season.

We were now in the last sixteen, three games from the Empire Stadium, Wembley!

The draw gave us mixed feelings, away to Cammell Laird, who had proved such a stumbling block in the past. They played in the West Cheshire League supposedly a lower standard and it was rumoured they paid subs to play. I can still remember struggling to get to sleep the night before, repeatedly going through the strength of our team and thinking there's no way we can lose this one.

How wrong I was! We simply froze and never looked like winning. In front of a crowd of 700 a 4-2 winning score didn't flatter the home side. It was my biggest disappointment since joining the club more so because we all knew we had the capability to go on and win the trophy.

One of the most horrible parts about helping run a football club, at least it is for me, is parting company with a manager and that is how I felt when we met with Russ at the end of the season. We had enjoyed so many wonderful memories with Russ and you feel an absolute jerk when you are effectively telling him he is being sacked. Russ clearly thought we were idiots with far too high an expectation of what we could expect to achieve on our gates and with our budget. Russ would never compromise on the way he wanted to play football and was admired throughout the north west for that. You could not but respect his principles and I was so sorry to see such a decent football man leave us. However, being absolutely honest I felt if we were to become league title contenders we needed to learn from the success of Atherton LR and aim for something part way between their mind numbing defensive obsession and the expansive football Russ had provided us with.

'A LITTLE APPREHENSIVE'

The Victoria Park ground and playing area was an absolute credit to the club in those days. It was the kind of traditional non-league ground I loved, situated just off the village centre and approached down a road of terraced houses, Prescot Cables' Hope Street ground was a bit the same.

One thing chairman Frank Parr would never compromise on was spending money on the playing surface immediately the season ended. He always used John Mallinson of Ormskirk one of the top sports field contractors in the country having worked on the City of Manchester Stadium, Old Trafford, Goodison Park and Liverpool FC's Melwood Training Ground. The pitch also had an enviable reputation for good drainage, very rarely was a home game called off due to rain.

With Russ now gone John Davison had been appointed manager. John lived in Burscough and had an unmatched record in non-league football having played almost 700 games for Altrincham and won 24 caps for England at semi-pro level. He had played for the Cheshire club in FA Cup ties against Liverpool, Everton and Spurs. With that kind of pedigree and at that kind of level it's fair to say I was a little apprehensive as to whether I could live up to the standards he was no doubt used to. Altrincham were a big club. His assistant manager was Peter King.

Well the truth was that John was very demanding and I had to quickly up my game and learn to do things his way. I have always in football been clear in my mind and to others that as a volunteer my days of taking shit from anyone ended when I left paid work so I was cautious about how our relationship would develop. However, that was not a problem with John. I soon saw that he was very professional in all he did and could see how the club was going to benefit from his experience and although there were occasionally one or two words thrown about I came to have a good working relationship with him if not quite as friendly as with Russ.

What was to follow over the next few years was the stuff of fiction!

At the end of last season I had seen a lad called Lee Trundle play for Liverpool County FA youth side in the national FA County Youth Cup Final against Essex at Burscough. I thought him a real talent. After the game there was a dinner at the Beaufort Hotel with some of the FA bigwigs present. Lee was sat close by and I got his phone number. He was on Liverpool's books but got released and went on to sign forms for Southport, playing in their reserves.

I told John about him and he asked me if I could get him up for a trial game on the ground. I drove to Huyton where Lee lived with his nan Josie, picked him up and brought him to Burscough. I deliberately stood on the far side of the ground away from the technical area but during the game John came round and asked me what I thought. I told him I was impressed and I was. John seemed unconvinced as it was only a trial game and sensing his lack of enthusiasm I am a little ashamed to admit I lost it a bit and said: 'Well, if you want my honest opinion John, I think he's fucking brilliant.'

To be fair John then went to quite a bit of trouble to get Lee signed on non-contract forms for the club. Later on I lost it again!

Anyone who was at Victoria Park on the evening of Tuesday 26th September 1995 will never forget the sight of Trundle scoring four spectacular goals in a 4-2 win over Blackpool Rovers. John subbed him near the end and what a reception he got leaving the pitch. There that night were a large Southport contingent including director Barry Hedley and manager Billy Ayre. They had clearly come to see Trundle, he was registered as a player with them as well. I went on and on that we needed to get him on contract before he left the ground but nothing happened. I was fuming. I learned later from Barry Hedley that they tried everything to get Billy Ayre to do the same that night but he remained intransigent. How lucky we were. We finally got Lee signed up two days later and within six weeks had sold him to Chorley for seven thousand quid!

Trundle of course went on to become a cult figure at Swansea City several years later and was at one time transferred to Bristol City for £1 million. The fans called him Magic Daps because of his trickery. As I write he is club ambassador for Swansea and heavily involved in community work for the club. I am delighted that he has made such a success of his life.

By November a 7-0 win at Salford City took us to the top of the league. Terry McPhillips another ace scorer signed from Nantwich Town got a hat-trick. Among that team were Neil 'Jocky' Hanson, Ged Nolan, Billy Knowles and keeper Paul Blasbery all of who went on to give such loyal service to the club.

We'll return to Jocky later in our Mills and Boon spot!

The biggest change we saw in John Davison's first season was defensively, conceding just 40 league goals, only champions Flixton bettered that. I still recall one of the early season games at St Helens hearing John shout to Andy Howard: 'Get back behind the ball then take a rest.' I liked the sound of that. We went on to finish fifth.

Once more we were back at Gigg Lane in April to again contest the League Cup Final. Champions Flixton were the opponents so began strong favourites. Although without strikers Terry McPhillips, who had left, and Mick

McDonough, injured again, Andy Howard ran their big defenders ragged that night and was unlucky not to be credited with the only goal of the game, his shot seemingly going in off Phil Farrelly's arse. So after only ever playing two games with the club Farrelly's name went down in the record books. It was a good way to finish as the club completed fifty years with a trophy to round off John Davison's first season in charge.

'IMAGES OF NUBILE YOUNG WENCHES'

My first three seasons had been packed with excitement but on a personal level this was to be the most exciting of all. Now approaching the club's fiftieth anniversary I decided to research and publish a club history book.

Once I get enthusiastic about something there is no stopping me and I used to literally spend hours going through the archives of the Ormskirk Advertiser. I decided the book would go right back to the nineteenth century when the original Burscough FC was founded then through the Burscough Rangers years, they were very much the predecessors of the present club. I find that kind of research fascinating and it would become another regular feature of my 'retirement.'

My contribution would be based on this research so I asked local journalist John Yates who had supported the club all his life to write what would effectively be an eye witness account of those fifty years for inclusion in the book.

I decided early on that the title would be 'Green Village Heroes'. I was quite pleased with that as the club had always played in green. Unfortunately it was often to get misquoted as Village Green Heroes giving it a completely different connotation, conjuring up images of nubile young wenches dancing around a maypole. Well it did for me!

I was also granted special access to the photo archives of the Liverpool Echo in the city centre. I recall going in one evening and spending overnight going through files and finding some real gems for the book, leaving early the next morning. Sally must have wondered where I was. There must have been a team picture for almost every one of the fifty years. Les Rawlinson was on duty that night and he was almost as enthusiastic as me, he could not have been more helpful.

The launch of Green Village Heroes in The Barons

Much of my research involved talking to some of the older residents of Burscough who were able to supply me with more pictures and stories for the book. That was a really enjoyable part of my research and it also gave me the idea for another book of Burscough in old photographs that would be published a year or two later.

Between researching and writing up the book and my club duties I was now spending an inordinate amount of time on football related activities. I don't really know looking back if Sally was just patient or pleased though she never complained, she was always very supportive. Certainly it had taken over my life in so many ways, there may have been other things we could have done as a couple that were being neglected. We had two Shetland Sheepdogs (Shelties), Jess and Meg, but the kids were grown up now so our time was pretty well our own. It is something I have thought about in later years, wondering if I was plain selfish in devoting so much time to football rather than going out and finding another paid job. I lost Sally late in 2015 so I guess there is no point torturing myself now.

One of my favourite away games was at Chadderton near Oldham. Their secretary Dave Ball used to edit their programme 'Chaddy Chatter.' I always had a good rapport with Dave, in fact he wrote in the programme on our visit 'welcome to Stan Strickland and his fellow committee members'! Some of the stuff he wrote was hilarious, often taking the piss out of his own players though not in a cruel way. I still have the programme from 1995-96 season against Burscough. He was bemoaning the last game between the two sides when Chadderton had suffered a 5-0 home defeat. '55 turned up to watch our worst performance for several seasons and Sue had to hide all the knives in the tea bar as people were threatening suicide and trying to jump off the floodlight pylons. Not a good night for Chaddy fans. Our team, no bugger it, some of them are still alive and I won't embarrass them by naming them, other than Lee Spratt, who was a non-playing substitute and could not be faulted on the night.' Describing a great save by his keeper: 'There was just a blur of hair gel, talc and cycle shorts as he shot across goal.'

It was at Chadderton where I was due to give a live match update on a new radio station, Dune FM, who were based in Southport. When they came through the signal wasn't good so I set off up the stairs of the clubhouse hoping to get better reception while complaining 'I'll be bloody knackered by the time I get up here' only to be told I was live on air! Apparently, it went down quite well in the studio.

'A TRULY WONDERFUL EVENING'

It was decided during the season that we would hold an Anniversary Dinner in celebration of the club's Golden Jubilee I think it's called. Initially Frank appeared to favour selling tables to sponsors but I was strongly of the opinion that this should be about the players and officials who had served the club over that period. The response we eventually got was quite staggering.

My major job was to start contacting as many players and officials as possible from the club's past. I put adverts in all the local papers asking former players to get in touch. Often a player was still in contact with others and would pass the word on. It fitted in well with the club history book I was hoping to have ready before the dinner.

We decided the dinner would be held at the Burscough Royal British Legion Club in Lord Street. Canon Reg Smith who was the Rector of Bury and vice-chairman of Bury FC agreed to be one of the after-dinner speakers. He was well known on the circuit and came highly recommended by our friends in football.

At that time well known comedian and actor Freddie 'Parrot Face' Davies was the owner of the Lathom Slipway pub with his wife Vanessa. It was situated just outside Burscough on the Leeds-Liverpool Canal. He was approached to also to be one of the speakers and agreed, I think for a fee of £200, which must have been a great deal less than if we had booked him through an agent. He turned out to be worth every penny.

It was not as easy to get a book printed in those days, now it is very simply done online. Because it was only an order for 1,000 copies I used a company in Ipswich which meant two overnight stays in Suffolk to meet with the printers and finalise the layout. I covered all my considerable expenses in book sales and there was a bit left for the club. On one occasion when I was down there I went to a small village pub near Ipswich and got talking to some of the locals. When I told them I knew Larry Carberry I didn't have to buy another drink. Larry lived in Burscough and is one of Alf Ramsey's title winning Ipswich Town legends and still very much revered in those parts.

My launch of 'Green Village Heroes' in The Barons was only a week or two before the dinner so I doubted many former players would appear as many were based in Liverpool but the turnout was just amazing.

I had sent Frank an advance copy of the book as I had dedicated it to him. I will never forget arriving early with Sally and seeing Frank standing outside holding his book. Frank was not always very expressive about his feelings but I could see the delight in his face. We sold many books that night with John Yates and myself signing copies if requested. When I look back at the highlights of my time in football that was one of the best on a personal level. I can still picture all those former players stood around the Barons clutching a book.

One request for a copy of Green Village Heroes came from Billy Morrey, Billy had played for Burscough in the fifties. After receiving his copy he sent me a nice letter of thanks. It ended with: 'One of my grandsons is with Everton's School of Excellence and plays for Liverpool Schoolboys under 12 team. He has just broken the schoolboy record for scoring with 73 goals. He is an excellent player. Look out for him in the future. His name is Wayne Rooney.'

Billy and his wife Pat lived in Storrington Avenue where I grew up and where my brother Brian still lived. In fact Brian regularly used to stop for a talk about football with Billy and had got to know him well.

Almost breaking a rib at 50th Anniversary Dinner

The dinner was a tremendous success. I recall walking into the Legion and being completely taken aback by the room. It was a mass of green and white. Whoever had laid out the tables deserved a medal, I so wish I had got a picture before the guests arrived. The turnout of players, managers and officials from all five decades was just incredible and I felt so proud that present were six of the team that won a treble way back in 1947-48; Allan Woolley, Tom Saunders, Wilf London, Matt Brennan, Jimmy Aspinall and Frank Postlethwaite. Ex-Burscough and Liverpool centre forward Louis Bimpson was also there as was the club's first ever goalkeeper Bill Meadow and some of the club officials from those early days like Dick Holcroft and Ronnie Barker. Sadly former England player Bob Langton had died a few months earlier. It was just amazing the turnout and although the Advertiser were there taking photographs I again wished we could have got a group picture of them all although it might have been logistically difficult there were so many. There were about 250 in the room that night.

Canon Reg Smith was really amusing with his anecdotes but I have to admit Freddie Davies made me laugh so much I nearly broke a rib as he went from some serious tales about his life in TV and films to that daft budgie thing he does. It was just hilarious.

I had written out Frank's speech to include mention of all those former players, managers and officials present. After the speech Kenny Spencer came up to me obviously annoyed as to why he and his players from the seventies had not been acknowledged. I had to admit Frank had jumped a paragraph missing out the tribute I had written. It was the only hiccup in a truly wonderful evening.

'A GLOWING TESTIMONY'

While researching 'Green Village Heroes' I came across many old team pictures of football in Burscough going back to the nineteenth century and had many framed for display in the boardroom. Previously the walls had been bare of anything. I am not sure my enthusiasm for this was shared as last time I went back to Victoria Park they had gone. Having said that I can recall seeing Frank occasionally discussing a picture on the wall with a visitor.

Now going into my fourth season I was making more and more contacts in the game and one that did us some favours was Jimmy Gabriel who brought a strong Everton reserve side up pre-season, I can recall Nigerian born striker Daniel Amokachi was a big draw in one game. He was great with the kids after the game laughing, joking and signing autographs. Colin Harvey also did the same for us, these games gave a massive boost to the club's finances. We also had Michael Owen, Steve Gerrard and Wayne Rooney play at Burscough as youngsters but they were not yet big stars so were not an obvious attraction.

I got to know Colin Harvey quite well as I often bumped into him when getting a newspaper in Aughton and we'd stop for a chat. I will never forget that shot of him on television deeply upset following the death of Howard Kendall leaving him the last of Everton's 'Holy Trinity' of Ball, Kendall and Harvey. There is a statue of them outside Goodison Park.

Striker Lee Cooper had joined from St Helens Town and he was really knocking them in along with Andy Howard. All action Tommy Knox was still with the club and local lad Michael Chandon was establishing himself in the first team squad after impressing in the youth team. Peter King as assistant manager was a real presence and a popular figure around the club. Being Liverpool based he brought many good players to the club. Peter was another who died far too young.

With no trophies and another fifth place finish in Division One it could be argued that very little progress was being made though there was a feeling we were building towards a real push for promotion.

I was now pretty well writing and editing the whole programme. It was time consuming yet something I enjoyed doing. The worst scenario was if we got three home games together, Saturday, Tuesday then Saturday again. It rarely happened but could be quite a challenge if it did. The programme also gave me a chance to spout off my opinions something I wasn't always shy about doing and which on one or two occasions got me into trouble. I've still got quite a few of those programmes and I don't mind bragging I thought I did a good job.

The club had sold their social club into private hands many years before and it was now The Barons run by Pauline and Brian Sewell. I loved going in the Barons after the game. Over a pint or two we'd celebrate if we had won and moan if we'd lost. Pauline and Brian were great hosts and the set up with Burscough memorabilia and TVs everywhere was perfect. To me it was very much part of the football club even though there were constant battles about the doors on to the ground being opened during a game. They did a lot to support the club and we held so many memorable fundraising events there. I can remember Ian St John, Nobby Stiles, Joey Jones, Norman Whiteside, Howard Kendall, David Fairclough, Duncan McKenzie and even Bernard Manning being some of the star turns at sportsman's evenings mostly organised by Mark Parr.

As secretary I had worked closely with John Davison for two years yet I can't say I really knew what he thought of me so I was astounded at the end of season presentation night when he thanked lots of people then finished by giving me a glowing testimony for the support I had given him. It gave me such a boost to hear those words from someone I so much respected, I have never forgotten.

'LET'S GIVE IT A GO'

Keith Crawford had joined the committee and not only did he bring some real brains to the outfit he brought a certain sartorial elegance as well, certainly stood next to me he did. Keith was a professor at Edge Hill College (now University) in Ormskirk. I remember he had a football pedigree from when he worked down south having been heavily involved with Frome Town FC in Somerset. I often gave Keith a lift to games and my reward on occasions was a Chinese meal after the game at the Peacock in Ormskirk. He was a great addition to the club as he talked calmly and sensibly at meetings when some like me were blowing off steam. He could blow off steam during games though! Keith now lives in Australia with wife Jenny although I still keep in touch through Facebook.

By this time Gordon and Sylvia Cottle were listed as committee members and Sylvia had been joined by Margaret Manuel, almost certainly the first time in the club's history two women were on the club committee. Ken Griffin was president, he had his own painting and decorating business that proved useful in the summer months.

Margaret ran the canteen after we were given a long lease by the council on the brick building on the ground that had been a British Restaurant during WW2. I usually put in an order for her to save me a sausage roll! She also ran bingo nights to raise funds. Margaret was another great addition to the club.

Sadly, I got a phone call from Rod Cottam when updating the book to tell me Margaret had died. I remember her like yesterday, she was such a big part of the club during those wonderful years.

Michael Clandon was signed on contract prior to the start of the season and this was featured on the cover of the matchday programme. Since John Davison had moved Michael to left back his game had become more structured and less liable to the ill-discipline that had let him down in the past. We were aware he had the potential to attract clubs at a higher level.

Frank didn't like a big fuss about anything and tended to not tell the press too much about club affairs while I favoured a more open approach, the press could do a good job in publicising the club in my view. The trouble was I did sometimes get carried away, my biggest weakness.

The Richard Batho incident I would guess irritated and embarrassed Frank as I took it all the way to UEFA.

Batho scored twice for Kidsgrove Athletic in the opening game of the season at Burscough as the visitors won 3-2. They were likely be one of our main rivals for promotion and soon afterwards we discovered Batho didn't have international clearance to play in England having played for Caernarfon Town in Wales.

I made an issue of it in the media after the FA only issued a fine and it became a lead story in the Potteries. Normally you would expect any points accrued while Batho played while not legally registered to be deducted so I emailed UEFA headquarters in Switzerland querying the FA decision. The reply I got while very polite informed me it was a matter for the national association.

We were to have another good run in the FA Vase made even more remarkable as it seemed to take us the length and breadth of the country. After comparatively local wins over Blackpool Rovers and Salford City (remember them?) it was up to the north east to face Easington Colliery. High up on the cliffs overlooking the North Sea two goals from both Robbie Cowley and Mark Wilde were enough to send us through to the second round where a comfortable journey through the leafy lanes of Cheshire brought a 3-1 win over Nantwich Town.

It was then back up to the north east again to face Stockton for what proved a real tough one, Andy Howard coming off the bench to score twice and rescue the game. In the fourth round the draw went open and out of the hat came Sudbury Town away. It was a long journey down to Suffolk so overnight accommodation was booked in Newmarket. Famous for racehorses many of the training stables are based there and it was a common sight to see stable lads and lasses on horses tipping their hat and wishing you 'good morning sir' as they passed. It is actually a very nice place. Sadly, we lost the game 1-0.

Our final away game was at champions elect Kidsgrove with promotion to what was then the UniBond League looking certain as the Staffordshire club's ground appeared unlikely to meet promotion requirements. It had been clear for a while that Frank had huge concerns about accepting promotion and was not looking a happy man. It is hardly surprising in a way, costs were bound to escalate considerably with higher wage demands and increased travel. Financial worries were never far from the surface and as chairman such problems usually ended up at Frank's door. I think it's fair to say everyone else at the club was enthusiastic about giving it a go and that's what I recall saying to Frank at Kidsgrove, let's give it a go and if it doesn't work out and we fall back down again at least we tried. I also reminded him of the work he had instigated on the ground to bring it up to promotion standard.

I am not sure my words helped but Frank did come on board, we accepted promotion and the incredibly successful years that followed more than justified that decision.

'INCREDIBLE WHAT WE ACHIEVED'

In early 1998 I suggested to the local council that the road immediately outside the ground leading to the sports centre should be named Bobby Langton Way. Bob Langton as he was known in the village had played eleven times for England and was undoubtedly Burscough's most famous son. I had researched and written a biography of Bob that for various reasons wasn't published commercially and it seemed right that his name should be remembered in the village. There was a naming ceremony outside the ground attended by family members and council officials. I am quite proud of my part in that though as I write I am not sure that sign will survive.

I just loved match days at Victoria Park, the whole place coming alive as everyone went about their duties. It really was like a well-oiled machine at Burscough.

I was normally one of the first to arrive at the ground. All the main facilities were under the stand so it was so quiet to start with then the gradual escalation of noise as players and match officials began to arrive, then, as kick-off approached you could virtually hear tensions building up with final instructions being barked out by managers and coaches.

I always made sure I was in position for the start of the game. I usually sat in the press area at the back of the director's box, often with journalist Geoff Howard, while keeping a match record. Sometimes I did the team announcements over the PA system. I used to dread being in charge of timing the 'Golden Goal' as I was always in danger of being distracted and forgetting to stop my watch.

I always had a good relationship with our neighbours Skelmersdale United, in fact I had been to some of their games during those successful FA Amateur Cup years including one game down south at Sutton United. Arthur Gore and Bryn Jones were particularly good friends and I got to know manager Tommy Lawson well, he had a mobile snack bar on the industrial estate where I would call for a sausage barm when back in Lancashire. It was certainly competitive when we met but both clubs shared many if the same problems and I always believed in keeping things friendly off the pitch.

In 1998 Stan Petherbridge returned to the club as treasurer, he had previously been treasurer before I joined. We shared an office and he was one of my main drinking partners in the Barons after the game. He more than anyone else I have kept in touch with since leaving the club. It was not a position in the club I ever relished. I lost count of the times we sat in silence at meetings wondering how the hell we were going to extricate ourselves from the latest financial crisis. All things considered it was incredible what we achieved.

One time I wrote about Stan acquiring near cult status within the local Asian community for his ability to down a chicken vindaloo after games at the village's Gandhi Restaurant. He usually went with Puskas, who I referred to as his minder, Puskas having already attained cult status due to his ability to down anything. Stan went on to try the restaurant's 'gunpowder' curry, resulting in not just his cult status going down the pan!

Michael Yates was a local Burscough lad who had grown up at Liverpool alongside Steven Gerrard and Michael Owen. After being released as a player he was offered a job with the club's academy. While still working at the academy he signed semi-pro forms for Burscough in 1998 and was soon scoring goals at an impressive rate so much so that he attracted the attention of a scout for Scottish Premier League side Dundee.

He signed for the Dens Park club with Burscough receiving a transfer fee of £12,000. Perhaps surprisingly for a club of their standing they asked to pay the fee in instalments explaining they had huge financial commitments developing their ground to retain their place in the Premier League. Michael went on to play in the Scottish Premier League before returning to Liverpool's academy where he now has more than 25 year's service.

Visit of Everton manager Walter Smith to Victoria Park

We seem to always have a good relationship with Everton. As well as Jimmy Gabriel and Colin Harvey doing so much for us their head of academy Ray Hall was also our good friend and it was him that suggested Burscough as a venue for Everton's academy games. He brought manager Walter Smith along to the ground to view the pitch and our facilities. He was obviously impressed as the arrangement went ahead. I think the main problem that arose was that many of the parents were not happy with their kids not playing on Everton's own pitches, the playing of games at Burscough had taken them away from the club. I could understand that so it didn't last long. We never made any money from hosting those games, it was only a bit of a prestige thing anyway.

Liverpool sent teams pre-season although hardly ever with any of their bigger stars. We were grateful because we still got a fair crowd. Even though I have supported the club all my life I never found Sammy Lee or Steve Heighway to be anything like as affable as the Everton lads we encountered.

We entered a reserve side in the Preston League this season with John Carberry as manager assisted by Steve Robinson. The good thing was that John knew John Davison well so was fully in tune with what was required. Managing a reserve team can be one of the most frustrating jobs in football if it is done properly often not knowing which players are available until the night before or even the day of the game.

Many clubs allow a reserve side to become a separate entity, winning trophies becoming more important than the club as a whole and supporting the first team. It is a complete waste of the club's money and was never allowed to happen at Burscough. It wasn't easy to run the kind of set-up as we had at Burscough and I know it tested John Davison's patience at times if he was drawn into some petty dispute within the club, he had enough on his plate with the first team. I think we did it better than most though.

Later we entered the reserve side in the Lancashire League, far better opposition and far better grounds. I saw in a programme dated February 2001 that 57 players had already played for the reserves that season giving some idea of the problems a manager faced!

Getting international clearance between say England and Wales was usually straight forward, the two FAs had a reciprocal arrangement, probably the only thing they ever agreed on. 48 hours at the most was the norm. It wasn't always so straightforward when an overseas FA was involved.

I particularly recall a player from the Cameroons that I was asked to get signed, I think it might have been John Carberry for the reserves. His name and the date are now long forgotten. The Cameroons by then had a good reputation having regularly qualified for World Cup final stages and their player Roger Milla had become something of an international celebrity. After a few weeks I had made no progress and the player was getting impatient. He must have phoned home as next thing the clearance came through and I was told that his mother had gone to the national association's head office in Yaounde and threatened an official with her umbrella. I like to believe this story is true.

Cries of hypocrisy might have been justified after the Batho incident when we learned our keeper Paul Blasbery had played several games for Burscough without international clearance. Paul had been signed from Hyde United but while with them had played one game on loan with Mold Alexandra in Wales. It appeared his registration had not been transferred back across the border. We only found out after Paul had been booked, for time wasting I think, and the forms went to the FA.

I told Paul the only way we're going to avoid losing points is for you to personally take the blame. It will lead to you being fined but the club would pay the fine. Paul agreed to this and wrote the perfect letter, the club avoiding censure. I believe Paul went on to qualify as a solicitor with the Crown Prosecution Service so it's perhaps hardly surprising he was able to get us out of the mire. Blas played over 300 games for Burscough having made his debut way back in December 1986. I recently learned from Pete Hill that Ged Nolan made over 350 appearances and I would guess Neil Hanson and Billy Knowles were right up there in those kind of figures.

'THE SACRIFICIAL LAMB'

Long coach journeys north became common once we joined the Northern Premier League but plenty of time for a few beers on the way home.

Blyth Spartans was always an experience. 400 of their supporters could be quite frightening, I've never heard language like it. One time our coach driver did not have a good day, in fact he had a nightmare day. When reversing at the Blyth ground he failed to see a metal pole which went straight through the back window with glass everywhere. Everyone had to move forward for a draughty journey home. Not only that some of the players were taking the piss out of his driving. When he turned off the M6 he stopped the coach, got out and refused to go any further until the players responsible left the coach. It could have been any of a number of players but keeper Matty Taylor was offered as the sacrificial lamb as he lived nearest in Parbold. In truth Matt was the one least likely to have been the guilty party. We never had that driver again, I think a joint decision.

Then there was the time we travelled to Gateshead only to see the match officials leaving the ground having called the game off. The pitch was frozen, it appeared communication between the football club and the staff at the International Stadium was non-existent. It was a soulless place as where all stadiums with a running track.

The facilities there were superb, they had everything you could possibly want except a kettle. We never even got offered a cup of tea before setting off home again.

A wet Tuesday night FA Cup game at Evenwood Town I recall, now that really was the back of beyond. Ryan Bowen covered every blade of grass that night, he'd just come back from Peru and we wondered what he'd been on!

We arrived at Spennymoor for one game and the pitch was pretty much afloat. Because of the distance we had travelled the ref said he would give it a go. It was all on the farcical side yet the game got finished. They had a good chippy nearby, that was my best memory of that game.

We always enjoyed playing at Gretna, our one trip into Scotland. Their hospitality in the boardroom after games was legendary with the wee drams flowing freely. They were really nice people especially secretary Ron McGregor and his wife Helen. Of course Gretna went on to greater things before it all went tits up. Ron was one of the few that remained with the club throughout all its ups and downs.

There was a bus stop at the top of the Rainford by-pass where the coach regularly dropped many of the players off on the way home, their cars parked nearby. They'd all pile behind the bus shelter for a pee, it's a wonder it didn't eventually fall over.

'SIGNAL OF A NEW ERA'

Since I had been at the club the youth team had been managed by Kevin Downey, first with Barry Beesley then with Frank Duffy. I always admired Kevin as manager. He had a great relationship with the young players yet was smart enough to outwit them if they got too clever. From the start I was very supportive of the youth team going to games whenever possible.

We had a good side then yet it used to annoy me the relationship Southport had with the people at Liverpool County FA, Joby Humphreys in particular. Through their youth development guy Dave Hughes I felt they were picking up the best young players out of Liverpool, always a rich seam of talent. We had heard Dave had become disillusioned at Southport so met up with him and convinced him to throw in his lot with Burscough.

Dave's arrival was the signal of a new era as we went on to build up the most successful youth set-up in the whole of English non-league football. We had already seen players like Ryan Bowen, Steve Perkins and Michael Clandon progress to the first team. Now we would see a whole lot more.

Dave was relentless in chasing up young talent. He also had good contacts with Lancashire FA, in particular Fred Southern who became a good friend of Burscough. Fred used to rave about our youth team and twice he arranged for them to represent Lancashire against the Scottish FA's national team, winning both. Fred was also very friendly with Bob Langton and when I was researching and writing a biography of Bob put me in touch with Tom Finney. I interviewed the great man over the phone, he was clearly a great admirer of Bob.

We represented Lancashire twice yet clearly there were

elements in their FA who were not happy about being represented by a team consisting mainly of Scousers. I suppose they had a point so we weren't asked again.

I remember our goalkeeper Paul Moore telling me about a striker in the Liverpool Sunday League team he managed. He told me he had mentioned him to John but that was as far as it had got. At the time we were training at Edge Hill College so I advised him to bring the player up with him to the following Thursday night's training, as I said to Paul, at worst John can only chase him away.

Ryan Lowe went on to be the UniBond League's leading scorer and one of the best strikers the club ever had. The problem was he would not sign a contract as he wanted to continue playing Sunday football so when Shrewsbury Town came in to sign him they didn't need to pay us a penny. Frank got on to their chairman and sweet talked them into agreeing a donation, £5,000 I think.

Ryan was another who went on to forge an incredible career in league football and as I write is manager of Plymouth Argyle having just led them to promotion to League One. His playing career has included Bury, Sheffield Wednesday, Crewe, Chester as well as Shrewsbury. A rival in Devon is former Burscough keeper Matt Taylor who is managing Exeter City. It says much for Burscough that we have seen so many of our former players go on to make football their full-time profession.

I recall sitting next to Joey Barton for ninety minutes in the stand at Victoria Park. He was only seventeen, a typical cocky Scouse lad. I found him good company and likeable, a word I would have struggled to use in later years. We were watching a Burscough youth game. Dave Hughes had brought him along and although then registered as an academy player with Manchester City he had begged Dave to play in the game.

Dave couldn't take the chance even though it was only a friendly. David Nugent did play in a friendly for our youth team before joining Bury and going on to play one game for England, in which he scored.

The day our youth team played Bootle at Victoria Park in the Liverpool County Youth Cup saw a big striker for the opposition make an equally big impression. I asked Puskas to try and get his phone number. How he managed this I don't know, but he did.

Bootle were actually using the players of a junior club, Brunswick, as their youth team. The players name was Lee McEvilly. Kevin Downey was keen to have Lee at Burscough in his youth team so following a phone call I arranged to meet Lee with his parents at their home in Netherton. I explained about the great youth set up we had at the club and our policy of offering talented young players a contract if we believed they were destined for higher things. I told them about our players that had already progressed to the professional game. It proved another success story when Lee agreed to sign for Burscough.

In October an FA Trophy game at home to Ilkeston Town was hardly memorable for the result, we lost 6-2, more so for an Ilkeston director storming into the boardroom at half-time accusing a spectator of racially abusing one of their players and threatening he would report us to the FA. Further investigation confirmed it was long standing supporter Ronnie Lawson, known as Tricky. Ronnie had one of the loudest voices in local football but what we learned he shouted wasn't very nice and I won't repeat it here.

My feeling was, get in there first, so 9.00 am Monday morning I was on the phone to the FA then at Lancaster Gate to tell them of the incident and ask how best we deal with it, I think it was Adrian Bevington I spoke to. I also phoned the Kick It

Out campaign headquarters in London for similar advice.

As a result I had no choice other than to write to Ron and tell him his behaviour was unacceptable and any repeat could lead to a life ban. As far as I know the Ilkeston guy did not report the incident and the action we took satisfied both the FA and Kick It Out.

Thinking about it later we did have some problems with our pensioners, Don Fraser, owner of a local coach company, once getting into an altercation with an opposing keeper at the Crabtree end. Then there was Barney!

Scarborough quite likely had never heard of Burscough yet within four years they must have been sick of the sight of us as three times we knocked them out of the FA Youth Cup. They were a big club having just been relegated from the Football League to the Conference the first time we went there in 1999-2000 season. Their chairman then was larger than life John Russell and even for a youth game he royally entertained us with superb hospitality in the club bar. Two years later we went again, Russell had gone, and there was a far more downbeat feel about the place. Within ten years the club had folded.

Russell went on to get involved with Exeter City, even on one occasion bringing singer Michael Jackson to the club, and was later jailed for fraud.

The youth team won the Lancashire Youth Cup for the first time with a 5-0 win over Old Blackburnians at Leyland. Manager Kevin Downey was delighted, he had described the competition as his Holy Grail.

'A TITANIC BATTLE'

1999-2000 was the season John Davison really put his stamp on the team who were becoming almost impossible to beat in league games, the only criticism perhaps being too many ending in a draw. We were rarely out of the top two all season and entering the final few weeks John D was forecasting we would need over 80 points to be in with a shout of promotion. He was to be proved so right as a titanic battle for the top two places went down to the final game of the season.

Burscough for many years had been blessed with some tremendous goalscorers and a strike force of Ryan Lowe, Mark Wilde, Lee McEvilly and Robbie Talbot was never going to leave us short of goals but once again it was the defensive record that had become such a feature of John Davison's time in charge that was providing the foundation, the best in the division by a distance.

One remarkable game during the season that might not have totally pleased John was a 7-4 win at Netherfield up in Kendal, Ryan Lowe scoring four with Billy Knowles, Ray Birch and Robbie Talbot also on target.

With such an exciting climax in prospect I recall making a fool of myself when I got annoyed with the Advertiser. I felt there were too many headlines about local cricket at a time we were in such a thrilling end of season battle for promotion to the UniBond League Premier Division.

I wrote about it in the programme and as a result was invited to go and meet with Geoff Howard and the newspaper's editor at their office in Burscough Street. Gordon Cottle came with me. I am not at my best when I lose my cool and I made a complete balls-up of presenting our case then ended up storming out...straight into a store room full of mops and buckets! Even now I cringe.

In truth I had nothing but respect for the job Geoff did in covering local football. The last thing you want is bland reporting that upsets nobody yet tells you nothing. Geoff was never afraid to tell it as it was so therefore always well worth reading.

We went to Harrogate Town for the final game of the season knowing a win would make promotion a certainty. Anything less would mean Witton Albion would go up if they won at home. I will never forget the annoying idiot on their PA system who thought it would be helpful to keep announcing that Witton were winning. I think he was trying to wind us up, John Davison must have been fuming.

Billy Knowles put us ahead in the first half and Ryan Lowe got the second from the penalty spot after John Lawless, making his first team debut, had been fouled, Burscough going on to win 2-1.

It was a marvellous achievement on one of the lowest playing budgets in Division One, exactly what we had hoped for when appointing John Davison. John had taken Burscough to heights never before seen in the club's long history. Not only that, we never lost one away game all season and only lost two in total. We missed out on being champions to Accrington Stanley on goal difference and finished ahead of Witton Albion on goal difference, all finishing on 84 points. That's how close it all was.

In eight years we had gone from the bottom division of the North West Counties League to the top division of the Northern Premier League.

'NO WAY ON GOD'S EARTH'

In 2000 the decision had been made to offer shares and for the club to become a limited company. Previously we were an unincorporated association run by a management committee. It was not a subject upon which I was very conversant so Dave McIwain explained to me that as it stood we as committee members could be personally liable for any debt the club might accrue. It was a time when some cases of injured players suing clubs for compensation had begun to surface. You were talking large figures. I could not possibly continue to leave myself and my family exposed to that kind of liability

The forming of a limited company would leave me as a director limited to a maximum personal liability of £1! At that time I felt I had two choices, resign from the committee and the club or accept the change to a limited company.

I believe we made about £12,000 from the share issue. I am of the opinion most thought of it as a donation to the club for which they would receive a nice certificate showing them to be a shareholder. I actually designed the share certificate. The only shares with real voting power were the 'A' shares issued to the directors thereby giving them control.

Becoming a limited company, however, was the moment the club left itself exposed to a possible predator!

In fact I was to discover virtually by accident that despite being secretary for eight years I was not to be offered a position as director at all. As I recall Frank Parr, Dave McIlwain, John Moorcroft and Rod Cottam would have been the four directors. Dave McIlwain and John Moorcroft both ran their own businesses so I am certain could offer far more than myself if financial backing for the club was the major consideration.

Someone, possibly Rod, must have told them that Stan will walk out of the club tomorrow if he is excluded, and I would have. No way on God's earth was I going to be a 'worker' reporting to a board of directors, my days of reporting to anyone were long gone. It was not just me it affected of course there were the rest of the committee. Eventually myself and Stan Petherbridge were offered positions 'on the board.'

I have little memory of this after all this time but Stan Peth reminded me recently that we actually signed up as directors in Martin Gilchrist's office in Southport!! The more I learn even now the more I wonder what was going on behind my back in those days and just who was doing what!

Martin Gilchrist had previously joined the club along with Dave McIlwain. They both agreed to put £5,000 into the club, Dave did, Martin didn't. After several promises that were never met we asked him to leave. Gordon Cottle used to say trying to pin him down was like trying to pick up a blancmange with your hand. What happened later with Martin Gilchrist was after my time so I can't comment.

It was all very unsatisfactory and I compounded it by putting out a press release. A mistake, Sylvia and Gordon Cottle only learned that they were not included this way. After all their service they were disgusted and left the club never to return. Gordon in particular had been a good friend and it remains a regret to this day. Vice-chairman Stuart Heaps also had every reason to be upset.

It was all handled very badly.

'THE BEWILDERED BETTERWARE SALESMAN'

Life was bound to get far tougher in the Premier Division though we got the perfect start with a 1-0 win over Hyde United in front of a near 300 crowd at Victoria Park, local hero Ryan Bowen the scorer.

A good FA Cup run saw Burscough reach the fourth qualifying round and after a home draw with Radcliffe Borough it became known the winners would be at home to Third Division York City. Unfortunately the replay at Radcliffe kept being postponed due to bad weather and both clubs were forced to make arrangements for the York game without knowing if they would be involved.

At Burscough we had to meet with the police to confirm we could hold the game safely at Victoria Park including having arrangements in place to segregate opposing supporters. That went off OK but then we were faced with having the expense of getting tickets printed without any certainty they would ever be used. Even more of a pain York wanted to have their allocation of tickets from both clubs so they could put them on sale immediately their opponents were known, time was moving on. So, one wet and windy midweek night I found myself on the M62 heading into the Pennines to hand over the tickets to York City Secretary Keith Usher at a motorway service station. Unfortunately, that was it, we lost the replay.

We were seeing more and more players coming through from the youth team, Matt Taylor taking over in goal from Paul Blasbery, while Tommy Molloy, Steve Leahey, Marvin Molyneux, Lee McEvilly and John Lawless were just a few now featuring in the first team justifying all the work that had gone into youth development at the club.

With Ryan Lowe gone Robbie Talbot and McEvilly really

came into their own this season. We also signed Stuart Rudd from Skelmersdale United where his scoring record had been quite phenomenal although he was never able to reproduce that form at Burscough. Andy McMullen was also providing an outstanding presence in central defence alongside long serving Ged Nolan.

We had virtually pinched Robbie Talbot off Marine where he had not exactly set the world on fire though it went on to prove something of an embarrassment for their long serving manager Roly Howard as under John Davison he became a prolific goalscorer with Burscough. So good a striker was he it came as no surprise when Morecambe came in with an offer o just under £10,000 early in 2001 that was accepted and the Christie Park club well got their money's worth as he carried on scoring goals at Conference level, scoring four on his debut, and later being selected for England at semi-pro level.

I drove up with Robbie to Morecambe following the transfer agreement to finalise the paperwork. I recall Robbie changing into training kit, I don't know if he worked out but you could see that upper body strength that was such a feature of his game enabling him to hold off defenders in a crowded area and get his shot away. He was given an address to go to locally for a medical. I must have then driven home as I only learned what happened later from the Morecambe website. I quote:

'Robbie Talbot was due to turn up at the club doctor's house for a medical after signing from Burscough. At the appointed time a man in a replica football shirt knocked on the door. The doctor answered and invited the young man in to wait. After waiting five minutes the doctor asked the man to come through to his surgery to 'start the medical.' The young man, startled, pointed out to the doctor that he was a Betterware salesman and didn't need a medical. Just after the bewildered

Betterware salesman left, Robbie Talbot knocked on his door.'

For much of the season we were in the top half of the table before finishing just below in 15th place, a not unsatisfactory start to life in the upper echelons.

'THE DELIGHTFUL BELINDA'

I recall us playing Scottish League side Stenhousemuir in a pre-season friendly. I got a call from top referee Mark Halsey requesting a couple of passes. Apparently he was friendly with one of their directors. The game proved a feisty affair ending three each and I thought the young referee handled it well. The ref told me later Halsey went in their changing room after the game and started giving a critique of his performance without introducing himself. 'I hadn't got a clue who he was. I just turned to him and said who the fuck are you?'

We also had a visit from famous Scottish side Queens Park. I had a former work colleague, Gordon Forrest, who was from near Glasgow and played the bagpipes. I arranged for him to come along with a mate and pipe the teams out. Margaret also put on haggis and neeps in the snack bar and that proved a sell out. I had some myself and it was really tasty.

The Scottish club's directors were genuinely delighted with our efforts but couldn't promise us a return game at their ground, Hampden Park!

2001-02 season began in great style as we won the Liverpool Senior Cup for the first time ever with a 1-0 win over Southport. It was actually held over from last season so bad had become the problems arranging these games. In front of a crowd of 520 Lee McEvilly scored the only goal to secure the impressive trophy for the Victoria Park boardroom.

And now to that Mills and Boon spot I promised. Neil 'Jocky' Hanson was a Bootle lad and a full back with Burscough for several seasons. Occasionally he was asked to play up front, this usually led to him turning his collar up Eric Cantona style. Belinda Manuel was a lovely, young, unsuspecting Burscough lass who helped out in the snack bar at the ground where she was chaperoned by her mum Margaret. Lured into the clutches of this scheming Scouser Belinda eventually fell for his dubious charms and married Neil, the loving couple settling in Burscough. Despite our concerns for the delightful Belinda I have to admit it has proved the perfect match and one of the club's great success stories!

I remember taking Lee McEvilly to Leeds United's Thorp Arch Training Ground near Wetherby where we were introduced to their manager David O'Leary. I cannot recall after all this time what Lee did there, I think at the most he took part in a training session, but the Yorkshire club never followed up their interest.

I far better remember our trip to Rochdale in December. I went with Lee and his mum and dad in their 4 x 4. The transfer fee of £20,000 had already been agreed between the clubs so it was now down for Lee to agree personal terms and sign. Rochdale's manager by then was John Hollins the former Chelsea player. He met us with his assistant in his office overlooking the ground. Terms were soon agreed my only real input being to suggest some built in bonuses based on appearances suggesting the more appearances the more Lee was a success. They readily accepted that.

The Rochdale fans soon shortened his name to Evil!

116 days after signing Lee became the first Rochdale player to ever win an international cap when he played for Northern Ireland against Spain at Windsor Park, Belfast. It had been discovered he had an Irish grandparent! I remember him telling me he swapped shirts after the game with Real Madrid's Iván Helguera.

I really liked John Hollins and he became a good friend of Frank even accepting an invitation to be our guest at Victoria Park for a game. What I couldn't understand that as a southerner with his family still living down London way was how the Rochdale job could be so appealing. He told me he travelled up and down the country every week between home and work. I guess you just have to go where the work is.

Barnsley had tried to scupper the deal by phoning Lee's parents on the morning of the scheduled signing at Rochdale. We threatened to report them for an illegal approach and they agreed to give us a pre-season friendly. They sent their reserve team, we struggled to cope with the crowds for that one!

Lee's mum and dad were just two of the parents that supported the young players at the club. They were good friends of Karl Clark's mum and dad and one holiday they took together abroad led to tragedy when Karl's dad Steve collapsed and died. Not that long afterwards Karl lost his mum Jan as well. I am still in touch with Karl on Facebook and his mum and dad would be so proud of the lovely family he now has. Karl was another that progressed through from the youth team to make his first team debut, one of many. Like me he is from Croxteth.

'WE KIND OF MET BERNARD MANNING'

Being involved in a club such as Burscough it was inevitable that you would encounter some well known names. I can recall three former international managers coming to Burscough; Scotland's Walter Smith and Craig Brown and Northern Ireland's Billy Bingham. Walter Smith I have already spoken about though I have no idea how the other two came to end up in West Lancashire.

We met Jackie Charlton in the boardroom at Blyth Spartans, his son John was manager. Stan Petherbridge remembers Jackie spoke to John Lawless sympathising that it was a long way home when you've lost. We kind of met Bernard Manning in the boardroom at Radcliffe Borough, his son Bernard Manning Junior was chairman. He just sat there in an armchair and spoke to nobody. It was the same when he was booked at the Barons, straight in, did his spot, paid and straight out. No socialising at all.

A well known figure from the soap Brookside came to do a charity event at our ground for a baby that had a disfigurement. His name was John McArdle, he played Billy Corkhill, and I happened to mention Brookside which I never watched and he reacted quite sharply telling me he was an actor suggesting he was known for much more than a soap series. It's true he has appeared in every British TV programme known to man.

Over the years we have had some famous players visit us as spectators. I recall Manchester City's Yossi Benayoun at one game, he also played for Liverpool. One of the players on the pitch was Israeli and must have been a mate. There was a lad in Mart Lane just across from the ground who had a window full of Man City pictures, obviously a huge fan. As Yossi was leaving the ground we tried to get him to go and knock on this guy's door and see his reaction but although he was laughing we couldn't get him to play ball.

What you won't find in any of Steve Gerrard's books is the time he came to Victoria Park with some friends to watch a Liverpool game in which one of his best mates Ian Dunbavin was in goal. While the game was on Gerrard and friends let down the tyres on Dunbavin's car. Quite how all that panned out I have no idea but I doubt he would have been too happy.

One thing I never expected to see was a player with 62 England caps tucking into pie and peas in the Barons after a game. Chris Waddle at the age of 40 had signed for Worksop Town. He came over as very much one of the lads after playing at Victoria Park. It wasn't just a gimmick either he played 60 games for them.

'THE BEST MANAGER THE CLUB EVER HAD'

Requests for complimentary tickets to games could be a dilemma. There were so many around who claimed to be official club scouts yet never appeared to do sod all for the club. There was one regular who had a Manchester United coat and pass though I often wondered how bona fide he was. Sometimes they might also request a reserved parking space, good luck on that one around Victoria Park.

Our visits to Accrington Stanley were the stuff of legend. Trying to gain entry to their ground would have made a great reality show. They were a most peculiar bunch, I think every one of them had been drilled by their chairman Eric Whalley to stop anyone getting in without paying and that sometimes included our manager, our players and even our kit having trouble getting past them, think East German border guards. Geoff Howard was covering one game for the Advertiser and was having a drink in the boardroom only to be told to 'sup up and get out lad', the nearest they ever came to a charm offensive. It was little different at reserve and youth games, I cannot recall a less hospitable club.

In 2001 the club held a sporting evening at the Scarisbrick Hotel in Southport. There was a comedian but the major attraction was former American heavyweight boxer Earnie Shavers who had once put the great Muhammad Ali on the floor.

Earnie was now living on the Wirral with his partner and her brother was his manager so I recall us travelling across the Mersey to meet Earnie. Jeez, he was a big lad! Like so many of those black boxers from the US he was a great talker, not that different from Ali. The evening began with some filmed highlights of his career including the Ali knockdown (of course Ali got up and won) but Shavers main claim to fame was that he had been voted the heaviest one punch fighter of the twentieth century. At the time he was working as a greeter at Yate's Wine Lodge in Liverpool. I bought his book and got him to sign it for me. It was a really enjoyable evening, I think organised by John Moorcroft.

2001-02 season brought the shock of John Davison's resignation in March when he informed us he and Peter King were moving to St Helens Town. Although in a lower division St Helens had exciting plans including moving to a new ground and it wasn't difficult to understand why this new challenge had attracted John and Peter. I believe their playing budget was considerably higher too.

John's leaving was a surprise and yet it wasn't, the atmosphere in the club had gone flat, I believe John had sensed it was time to go. If I am honest we didn't give the John the support he deserved at that time and didn't fight hard enough to keep him. I actually think we had become blasé after our previous success. We were lying sixth in January and tenth when he left….in the UniBond League Premier Division for God's sake, what more did we want? I was as much to blame as anyone and I remember writing to John expressing regret at our lack of appreciation, well mine. Things kinda went into free fall after he went and we finished nineteenth.

Supporters, me included, will forever talk about what happened the following season and what John Davison did for Burscough can too easily be forgotten. He had taken Burscough to its highest ever level with two promotions and to me he was the best manager the club ever had and that remains my view today. Liam Watson might have taken the club one step higher in later years but he never had anything even close to the budget constraints John had.

'A FOOTBALL MIRACLE'

When Shaun Teale joined us as player-manager at the start of 2002-03 season it was difficult to know what to expect, here was a guy that had finished second in the Premier League and was a League Cup winner with Aston Villa where he had become something of a club legend alongside his partner Paul McGrath. Although Shaun had played some games for Burscough as a youngster I guess the question was could he adjust to semi-pro football, could he adjust to us lot?

The question was soon answered, I found Shaun easy to work with, there was no air of superiority about him and he quickly adapted to the club appreciating we had some good youngsters and was prepared to give them a chance. With Ray Stafford as his assistant he brought a relaxed atmosphere to the club and the changing room especially of course as he was still a player himself. Then 38 he still made defending look easy and was to prove a huge influence especially in big games when he exuded a calmness that was infectious throughout the team. I also realised early on that though Shaun was famous as a player he was new to management so there were times when I could actually be of use to him!

The big news was the return of Gary Martindale to the club. I wrote prophetically in the first programme of the season: 'Gary has had some marvellous moments in the game since leaving Victoria Park, let's hope he has some more to come.'

It meant many of the 'old guard' moving on, some, not unexpectedly, to join John at St Helens. It was sad to see them go but I guess inevitable with the change of management though it now gave some of our younger players the chance to shine.

Right from the start Shaun had made it plain he was

ambitious to progress in management and that was never a problem to us. Progress would most likely come only if he had brought Burscough success so everyone would be a winner.

We could not have had a better start to the season, not conceding a goal in our opening seven league games and only two in the first eleven.

During the season I had an easy working relationship with Shaun. He was always very helpful to me, no request was too much trouble, always supplying his piece for the programme on time for example. I can only recall one time when I had a bit of a moan.

On my way home from holiday in Cornwall early in the season I phoned the ground for some reason. An unknown voice answered: 'Ello', nothing else. I said: 'Who's that?' It turned out it was the father of one of the under 17 youth players. It really pissed me off, we were Burscough Football Club and that's how we answered the phone yet this guy seemed to have suddenly been let loose around the club.

When I was next at training this guy was on the pitch with the players. It might seem a fuss about nothing but we had a definite hierarchy at the club where people had been appointed to positions within the structure we had, something you need if also having a reserve and youth set-up. It was always a delicate balancing act trying to keep everyone happy and throwing this loose cannon into the mix I could see leading to all kinds of problems. I can remember asking to have a word with Shaun and telling him of my concerns. Fair play to Shaun, we never saw him again.

I hope I don't sound too full of my own importance though it is true that you do build up something of an ego when involved with a club like Burscough. I am saying that because there were times when I was quite rightly pulled up. I remember one of the stewards, Barry I think, having a go at me for the way I spoke to him for which I apologised. I recall something I said upsetting Sylvia Cottle and she reminded me not to get carried away 'just because you've signed a few books.' A cutting remark following the launch of 'Green Village Heroes.' Yes, I did need bringing down at times.

After that great start to the season our league position gradually drifted down and down month by month but in the end who the hell bloody well cared as we went on to complete what has quite rightly been called a football miracle. Whether I have the literary skills to do that season justice remains to be seen!

For a club of Burscough's size to win such a prestigious national cup competition with 206 clubs entered including all 22 from the Conference while playing a total of 12 games along the way was beyond belief. Even today I sometimes find it hard to take in it really happened.

'PART OF CLUB FOLKLORE'

So many times during that incredible FA Trophy journey it could have all gone wrong. I remember us going to Marine in a first round replay. We had played them off the park but found ourselves a goal down with the game going into added time when Gary Martindale struck a volley from the edge of the area. He didn't get a clean strike on the ball and it looked an easy save for the home keeper but he fumbled the ball and spilled it over the line. We then went on to win easily in extra-time.

The more you remember about that season the more you look back in complete disbelief at the eventual outcome.

In February Shaun was told that the playing budget had to be reduced by about 50% with nine contract players being made available for transfer. I was part of that decision, the club being in a dire financial situation. I wrote in the programme: 'The truth is that almost five seasons playing in the UniBond League have finally caught up with us. We are a small club playing in a big league and nothing illustrates our problem better than the visit of Colwyn Bay. We were second in the league, playing some fabulous football and just 167 were present to see us give another spellbinding performance.'

Shaun was gutted but said he wasn't a quitter and would carry on!

Don't forget at that stage we were only in the second round of the FA Trophy so no-one could have foreseen what was to come.

Having survived against Marine we were just as close to going out in the second round when we went to Harrogate Town and with twelve minutes remaining were 2-0 down and all seemed lost. A Shaun Teale penalty gave us hope and with the game again in added time Joe Taylor swept the ball home to set up a replay that we shaded 3-2 thanks to two goals from Kris McHale.

We were drawn away to Ilkeston Town in the third round. It was played on a Tuesday night having been postponed on the Saturday. This was the game where young Drew Hyland made a big impact with his best performance for the club, scoring a fine opportunist goal in a fully deserved 3-0 win.

Here is where everything changed. We had put in a superb performance at Ilkeston and were now in the last 32 with prize money increasing by the round. I remember Roy Baldwin saying to me you just can't cut the wages now after that performance and while we are still in the Trophy. I couldn't but agree. Four directors had travelled to Ilkeston and back on the coach we decided there and then that we would have no part in a wage cut at that time a decision that did not go down well with some other directors who believed we had reneged on a democratic and binding decision. In principle they were right but the decision we made that night was the right one and went on to be proved so in a way that we could never have imagined.

Last time I spoke with Rod Cottam he claimed he played a big part in us being able to keep going financially during that period, I wouldn't know, but I do know Rod put his hand in his pocket on many occasions.

One of the draws for a round of the FA Trophy was held at Old Trafford. Frank and I went and Alex Ferguson came across from his office and made a short speech of welcome. I don't recall him being taking part in the draw. I think there were 32 teams in the draw so still a long way to go. Looking back what was funny was that both Frank and myself refused the opportunity to be pictured with the Trophy. At that time did we honestly think it would make a difference?

The two fourth round games against Alfreton Town stick in the memory because they were bad tempered affairs and they were by far the least sporting side we met on that memorable journey and predictably one of the few that didn't send us good wishes later in the season.

A home draw against Wakefield & Emley in the fifth round suggested a tight low scoring affair with both teams having good defensive records but we were devastating that afternoon and ran out easy 5-0 winners and even missed a penalty.

No matter what anyone else might have thought when we were drawn away to Yeovil Town in the quarter-final my feelings were well that's the end of the road but we'll get a good pay day.

What happened that day at Yeovil will always be part of club folklore. Yeovil by a big margin were the best non-league side in the country, runaway Conference leaders and destined for the Football League. As the holders they were determined to retain the trophy so there was no messing about from manager Gary Johnson as he picked his strongest possible side. The tactics of manager Shaun Teale that afternoon were nothing short of brilliant as he set out to defend the final third of the pitch like our lives depended on it and to cut out their supply of balls from the flanks.

For all our defending Matt Taylor was rarely forced to show what a good keeper he was and our counter-attacking with pace led to two great finishes from Peter Wright and John Bluck coming within inches of getting a third. The result sent shock waves through non-league football. I heard that when the result came through on the TV in the Southport boardroom chairman Charlie Clapham was not amused his club having not long been stuffed 6-0 by Yeovil.

The end of the game saw our players make their way over to applaud our band of supporters who had been joyfully doing the conga behind the goal and it was nice to see so many Yeovil supporters remain to the end and see our players clap them in appreciation.

As we left in our coach more Yeovil supporters applauded us out of the car park. A few beers were knocked back on the journey home and with the agreement of our regular coach driver Gary we pulled off the M6 somewhere in Cheshire to find a pub to further celebrate. We ended up pulling up at this small village pub. It was getting late and the landlord who was having a quiet night looked visibly shocked as we all piled in but credit to him as he got his wife and daughter out of bed and we ended up having a good session there.

We were in the semi-finals but there had not been much mention on the local TV stations. I bombarded both the BBC and Granada with emails reminding them of what this little village club in their area was achieving. I recall getting a phone call from a clearly exasperated Alistair Mann - now a Match of the Day commentator - saying they were preparing something and would I stop harassing them! In the end we did get good TV coverage although I've never understood why these TV companies think every non-league club ends with Town!

A two-legged semi-final with Aylesbury United was our reward. They had quite a set up at Buckingham Road where we played the first leg, at the time it was being used by the England team for training. A Gary Martindale goal gave us a 1-1 draw so everything now depended on the second leg at Victoria Park. Such was the tension at Burscough that it was in no way a classic but we rarely looked like losing without ever creating a lot of chances ourselves. Nobody will ever forget that incredible climax to the game as referee Eddie Ilderton awarded a penalty for a trip on Peter Wright in added time. It was a brave decision at such a late stage of such a big game but despite Aylesbury's protests video replays showed it was the correct decision, Craig Maskell having recklessly charged in with a typical forward's challenge.

I can remember almost praying that Shaun would take the penalty and as soon as I saw him grab the ball under his arm I just knew we were on our way to Villa Park. He was never going to miss and despite the delay and the tension he was laughing and joking with teammates. He fairly buried the ball in the net followed by crazy scenes of celebration around Victoria Park. It was another unforgettable moment in our small village club's incredible history.

I was so proud of the club that day. Our organisation was superb for such a prestigious occasion with a crowd of more than 1,700 and all kinds of bigwigs present. I can recall us forgetting to steward off the ref who was surrounded by Aylesbury players at the final whistle such was the excitement but otherwise we received nothing but compliments for the way we hosted such a big game.

'THE BIGGEST FAIRY TALE'

So we were in the FA Trophy Final and now the hard work really began. We along with Tamworth were summoned to go down to Villa Park to meet with the FA, West Midlands Police, Aston Villa secretary Lee Preece plus catering and ground safety staff, etc, to discuss the arrangements for the final. The FA's publicity machine really kicked off and one young lady whose name I have sadly forgotten became my main contact and particularly helpful and as the final got nearer I could tell that as she realised what a small club we were she was hoping we would win. I saw her after the final and the smile she gave me confirmed I was right!

We set up a ticket office in the canteen with Stan Petherbridge and myself on duty. Steve Clark the FA Competitions Secretary had told us that the previous season Stevenage Borough had sold tickets at random and their supporters were all scattered about. We didn't want that so Stan and I made the decision to sell the tickets from the centre line outwards both ways so that all our supporters were congregated together immediately opposite the Sky cameras and didn't that work well?

A special deal was arranged with Burtons in Ormskirk to supply suits and white shirts and they came along to measure us all up. I think Puskas set them a challenge! I can remember before we set off for Birmingham Shaun's wife Carol and Margaret in the boardroom ironing shirts. Everybody really mucked in.

We had a meeting at Shaun's house in Tarleton to further discuss arrangements. Shaun wanted to take the players down to Birmingham three days before the game to prepare. Although we had concerns that boredom might be a factor we agreed and the Holiday Inn nearest Villa Park was booked for the players and staff plus some club officials. Shaun and his wife had indicated that they wanted the players to stay in Birmingham on the night of the final and come home the following day. We understood that was the way they would do things with a club like Villa but we made it plain that if we won the Trophy we should come home the same night when excitement in the village would be at its peak.

I was so proud of how many of our former youth players were in the squad. Building up our youth set-up had been a passion of mine and I feel sure Dave Hughes would agree I gave him tremendous support. I used to watch every youth game home and away and some of my greatest memories at Burscough came from our exploits in the FA Youth Cup. I still never tire of telling people we had the most successful youth team in English non-league football at that time.

One of the nicest men I met in senior football was former Liverpool secretary Bryce Morrison who sadly died in 2009 aged only 57. I dealt several times with Bryce to make match arrangements when we met the Anfield side in the Liverpool Senior Cup or a pre-season friendly and he always treated us with the greatest respect, just the same I would imagine as he would treat a fellow Premier League club.

I remember him phoning to ask for FA Trophy Final tickets. Some of the Liverpool club officials wanted to go see the game, I think the number was twelve. I said I would come and drop them off at Anfield. Never one to miss an opportunity! I was shown up to Bryce's office and was invited to take a seat. We chatted for a few minutes then he asked me if I wanted a look around so I got a behind the scenes tour from the club secretary.

They did pay for the tickets!

We commissioned a video through two brothers, Martin and Alan Boardman, who had done such an excellent job of

Being interviewed at Villa's Training Ground

covering the Aylesbury game and they were with us throughout the three days we were in Birmingham and got some great footage. I had to negotiate permission from Sky to include the full match coverage and the commercial quality video they supplied cost us a few hundred pounds.

Shaun through his contacts had arranged for the team to prepare at Villa's Bodymoor Heath Training Ground. It was a superb facility and the staff looked after us so well. I feel certain those meticulous preparations played a big part in how we performed in the final.

The coach we had hired from Holmeswood Coaches for the whole time we were away bussed us everywhere. The driver Gary became very much part of the team and I bet he looks back on those three days in much the same way as we do.

While the lads were training Sky match commentator Rob Hawthorne came along to Bodymoor to familiarise himself with our players, recording what I was telling him and taking pictures. Rob is still one of Sky's top commentators, far better than Martin Tyler in my opinion, and his commentary of the game was brilliant with none of those patronising comments that non-League football occasionally has to suffer. He sent me an email following the final: 'Thanks for all your help leading up to the big day, and congratulations on your success. Thoroughly deserved!!' Rob's only slip-up was to have the Trophy presented to 'Carl McHale!'

Another brilliant thing about the final was the presence of about 400 players from the junior section in their Burscough shirts. It made quite a spectacle and really added to the day. Gary Wright and myself had put a great deal of effort into bringing Dynamo Burscough on board to be part of Burscough FC and Gary, Brian King, Steve Gamble and other junior officials were brilliant leading up to the final because there was a lot of work involved in getting all those kids down to Birmingham. It was so sad to learn while writing this book that Gary had died aged only 60, Gary and his wife Julie I remember as a lovely couple.

Villa Park looking good

The final itself in front of almost 15,000 spectators was something we will never ever forget. The proximity of Tamworth to Birmingham ensured our 2,000 fans were greatly outnumbered but by God did they make themselves heard! Gary Martindale in his second coming to Burscough was the hero and attained legendary status with the two goals that brought the FA Trophy back to this little Lancashire village. Watched live throughout Europe on Sky and in the clubs and pubs of Burscough it was hard to take on board just what we had achieved as the Trophy was presented by World Cup winner Martin Peters to Shaun and captain Carl Macauley.

Adjectives like sensational and unbelievable should be used sparingly or they lose their meaning but our win and the way we played that day was well worthy of either description. It was, and remains, the biggest fairy tale in the history of the FA Trophy.

I can't remember much of events at Villa Park after the final apart for loads of people coming up to congratulate us. I really was in something of a daze, it was all too much to fully take in. I had none of my normal after-match duties to do like phoning in the score and scorers to the league, press association, etc, so I just stood with a drink in the player's lounge hardly able to take my eyes off the trophy we had just won. Tamworth came in and you couldn't but feel for them but their club officials all came across to congratulate us.

'NOTHING IN MY WILDEST DREAMS'

The FA Trophy won we began the journey home. We were due to arrive in Burscough about 10 pm. A few days before the final I had arranged that Puskas would go on ahead, open the ground and switch on the floodlights and the PA system ready for the return. I might be a natural pessimist but I really couldn't believe that having reached the final we would now go all the way and beat a side that had just walked their league and were now a Conference club but I felt sure we would get a warm welcome whatever. Nothing in my wildest dreams could have prepared me for what I witnessed that night!

My wife had phoned me to tell me we were in for shock when we got back to Victoria Park. A further sign of what was to come came when the team coach pulled off the M58 at the Rainford By-Pass and there were two police cars waiting for us. They indicated that we should follow them. We travelled through Ormskirk town centre and I can still recall how quiet it was. It was the same on the A59 apart from the odd car that blew their horn as they saw the coach with the Trophy on display.

The sight I witnessed when the coach pulled into Mart Lane is something that will live with me forever. With the police car sirens blaring and lights flashing it was chaos of the nicest possible kind. The players were staring from the coach mouths wide open in disbelief at the crowd outside the ground. It took the coach about twenty minutes to get through the crowds so the players could enter the ground and then we saw the size of the crowd inside Victoria Park as well. There must have been close on 2,000 there that night. It more than anything brought home just what we as a club had achieved and was the perfect ending to that magical day.

The return home. Proudly holding the FA Trophy aloft with long time supporter John Spencer

The Barons must have been filled to three times capacity that night. You could hardly move and you certainly were lucky to get a drink. Supporters were going to pubs in the village to get drinks and bringing them back to the Barons. I can recall Peter Wright stood on a table conducting the Barmy Army. The atmosphere was just incredible.

The Trophy was being passed all around the Barons which reminded me of words spoken as we were leaving Villa Park earlier that evening. The FA's Steve Clark had come to me and with a certain pleading in his voice said: 'You will look after the Trophy won't you?' Solid silver and worth many thousands of pounds in previous seasons the Trophy had gone to big clubs like Yeovil, Colchester, Macclesfield, etc, and Steve knew it was now going to this little upstart Lancashire village club!! His concerns were perhaps justified as I looked around the Barons and thought to myself 'where's the lid?' Every effort to find the lid met with no luck, we even went looking all around the ground. Nobody could remember where they last saw it. I remember thinking oh God we've only been home a couple of hours and we've gone and lost the bloody lid. In the end it was found sitting on the head of someone fast asleep in a corner of the Barons and lid and trophy were reunited. Thinking about it now I hadn't got a clue where the plinth was either.

The camera team that had followed us for three days had not been present that night. Like us they could not have predicted those scenes. I was distraught that we had no record of that fantastic homecoming to include in the final video but someone told me they had seen a guy with a camera filming. Some detective work over the next few days traced the cameraman and it turned out he had been filming for Granada TV. He happily let us have footage to include in the video.

The celebrations went on for days. We set up a stall outside Graham's selling the final videos with the FA Trophy on display. Cars going past were honking their horns. The Trophy got taken into local schools by Stuart. It was taken round the local shops who had supported us with those fabulous window displays. We were given a civic reception by West Lancs Council and of course there was great coverage by Geoff Howard in the Advertiser.

I remember sitting at home one evening a few days after the final eating egg and chips with the FA Trophy in the middle of the table next to the HP sauce. It was that surreal and still hard to take in but what a wonderful few days they were.

We made more than £100,000 from the FA Trophy that season. Our share of the Yeovil gate came to about £18,000 then there was our cut of the semi- final games that attracted more than 3,000 spectators in total. There was the £35,000 Sky TV money and the prize money that increased through each round and our share of the final gate although that didn't amount to that much because of the massive overheads for a final at a ground like Villa Park.

Stan Petherbridge recently sent me a copy of the balance sheet. The gate money totalled £155,480, Tamworth and ourselves each received £12,873 as our share of the gate!!! Keith Crawford on seeing it exclaimed: 'Bloody hell, the band got nearly as much as we did.'

One thing that really irked us however was that the £25,000 that had been paid to finalists in previous finals as compensation because Wembley was unavailable had been withdrawn that season. I wrote to the FA pleading our case that the payment should be made especially as so much of the gate money from a 14,296 crowd had gone in expenses. The Tamworth chairman asked me for a copy of the letter and they sent it in as well. My pleading letter was successful and we got the £25,000 and so did Tamworth. To be fair we also paid out a lot during that epic cup run to ensure that Shaun and the lads got the best possible treatment including bonuses, travel and overnight stays for Yeovil, Aylesbury and of course the final. The money paid off all our considerable debts and as I recall left us with about £20,000 in the bank. The first time I could ever remember us being anywhere close to solvent.

Most of all the winning of the FA Trophy was a fitting reward for chairman Frank Parr in his 57th year with the club. It was marvellous to see him on the pitch celebrating with the players and being congratulated by spectators after the game. Frank taught me a lot about how a football club should be run and how standards at Burscough should never be compromised which I continued to use as my guiding principles after leaving the club. I will always have enormous respect for Frank.

As I write now it is over 17 years since that magical day and although I have experienced many more memorable moments in football since nothing will ever come close to matching what we achieved in May 2003. It really was a miracle.

'I WILL NEVER FORGET SALLY'S JOY'

One of my lasting personal memories of that day is of when Sally my wife phoned me on the team coach so excited and emotional about the scenes awaiting us at the ground. It was the same as we arrived in Mart Lane I could see her clapping her hands above her head clearly so delighted for me and Frank and the players. I think she always had a bit of a soft spot for Frank, she had a knack of making him smile through mildly jesting with him.

Sally had an enthusiasm for refurbishing old furniture and I can recall her doing a refurb job on what was the chairman's chair in the boardroom. It was a fine chair with some age and looked immaculate when she had finished and I always felt a certain sense of pride when Frank always claimed it for chairing meetings.

I had managed to get tickets in one of the hospitality suites at Villa Park for my eldest daughter Kerrie and two friends. They had a wonderful view from a balcony in one corner of the ground and she still talks about that incredible day.

It was a special memory for me to finally see my family getting such pleasure from my involvement in football, I will never forget Sally's joy that day.

I won't let false modesty get in the way of recounting that following our FA Trophy win I was honoured by the Non-League Directory with a National Merit Award. I was invited to a dinner at Telford United's New Bucks Head Stadium to receive the award from Directory editor Tony Williams. In truth I felt Shaun or Frank were more deserving of an award though I was happy to accept on behalf of club secretaries everywhere who rarely get an opportunity to steal the limelight!

I was also able to share with Sally the UniBond League presentation night at the Hilton Hotel in Blackpool at the end of that season. We had time to relax with a visit to Stanley Park in the afternoon before putting on our glad rags for the main event in the evening. Accrington Stanley had won the league but even that was overshadowed by our success at Villa Park. With the FA Trophy on display so many came across to congratulate us, you could not fail to feel so proud. It was a wonderful weekend, just more magical moments that I still cherish.

With my wife Sally in Blackpool

Trophy final referee Uriah Rennie made one amazing mistake by only playing 44 minutes in the first half. We tried to pull his leg about it that night yet he still wouldn't admit it even though there was proof on the Sky TV coverage. I thought him a little arrogant and humourless in truth although he had a stunning girlfriend with him. We soon lost interest in him if not her.

'A HUGE MISTAKE'

How did relations between Shaun and the club so quickly fall apart after the Trophy final?

I have to own up, I could well have been an initial part of it. I was having a drink in one of the restaurant areas of Villa Park before the final feeling relaxed having just given in the team sheet to referee Uriah Rennie, the last of my match day duties. Next minute Shaun's wife Carol came rushing in clearly wound-up and wanting to know where she took two mascots. I think it was her sister-in-law with her. I felt I was being accused of making a balls-up of the arrangements.

I always thought the logistics of getting the sixteen mascots together with the players would be one of the biggest challenges and I went to enormous trouble to ensure everyone with a mascot was aware of the arrangements. I issued an A4 sheet to every player with those arrangements right down to the finest detail. The partners of Gary Martindale and John Norman agreed to collect the mascots and liaise with the FA official who would escort them to the player's tunnel. Having gone to so much trouble I probably came over as unsympathetic and Carol stormed off. I called her 'sister-in-law' back and asked her to get Carol to calm down and get the mascots to the players tunnel which they obviously did. I don't really feel I did an awful lot wrong.

However, there was another incident during the game where I do accept the blame. With about twenty minutes to go and us two up I was a bag of nerves as the impossible was beginning to look possible. Michael White came on as a substitute and I couldn't help saying out loud 'it should have been Marvin.' Next minute Carol got up from behind me clearly furious and looking to move to another seat away from me.

Despite the fact I do get carried away during a game I should have been aware of Carol behind me and that my comment would be seen as criticism of Shaun. Shaun and Carol were very protective of each other and I can understand why my comment so upset her. It wasn't deliberate but I have always greatly regretted that happened.

Following the final there were strong rumours a former club Weymouth were going to offer Shaun the job of manager, he had been seen at Villa Park talking with their chairman Ian Ridley. We had always been aware that he was keen to progress in management so it wasn't a problem although there was a feeling he was already turning his back on us.

Shaun going partying with friends after winning the Trophy instead of coming home on the team coach was a huge mistake. We had advised against it and been ignored. It was disrespectful to the club, the supporters and to his own players and although he was there the following night when BBC and Granada reported live from the ground the moment had passed, those incredible scenes of the previous night's welcome home gone forever.

Supporters had arrived home from Villa Park. Others had been watching our win on TV in pubs and clubs in and around Burscough. There was near hysteria in the village and coming home that night with the Trophy was one of the best decisions club officials ever made. I am repeating myself I know but those scenes will live with me until the day I die.

We had done everything Shaun wanted to make preparations for the final as perfect as possible. Why couldn't he have gone along with the one thing we asked? I will never understand, we should all have been celebrating such a magnificent achievement together. He was our hero, he had made the impossible come true. I've said it until I am blue in the face, we would never have come within a million miles of winning the FA Trophy if Shaun had not been our player/manager.

My feelings today sat here writing this on the Isle of Anglesey are of nothing but gratitude towards Shaun for giving me my greatest day in football and the words I have written are because I am sad about what happened, it should have been so different. I would love to have a beer with him and reminisce about that sensational season but it just ain't gonna happen.

By the time we had a civic reception in Ormskirk things were very cool between Shaun and club officials and by the time of a Supporter's Club presentation event in the Barons they were downright toxic. Frank certainly didn't deserve his treatment when receiving an award.

I'm not sure of the order of events now but we had a meeting with Shaun and Ray Stafford in the social club on the ground in an effort to resolve some of the issues. I remember Shaun saying he wanted to speak to me later, presumably about what happened with Carol, though he never did. Maybe if he had it would have been productive, I just don't know. I understood he would feel bound to support Carol. I gave Shaun and Ray a copy of the Trophy Final video but I don't recall anything being satisfactorily resolved during that meeting and the atmosphere remained strained.

'TIME TO CALL IT A DAY'

Not long afterwards I resigned as secretary and as a director but the way I did it was one hundred per cent wrong. I sent a letter of resignation to Frank and Geoff Howard at the Advertiser and typically it got to Geoff first. He phoned Frank about my resignation and Frank had not a clue what he was talking about. It was so unfair on Frank, I should have spoken to him about my feelings rather than sending those letters.

That season had been exhilarating and had ended with that wonderful day but I think also left some of us feeling quite exhausted. I had been secretary for eleven years and much as I used to look forward to a new season I just knew I had got to the stage where I could no longer face starting another season arranging friendlies and officials, registering players, sending off entry forms, etc. I knew it was time to call it a day. The Shaun Teale situation didn't help yet it was not my main reason by a long way.

After sending out those letters I suppose it was inevitable later that morning that I saw Geoff walking up our garden path. I guess I unloaded all my thoughts to him and of course it ended up being a big story in the Advertiser.

I remember Shaun saying when I resigned it would lead to him being sacked and as soon as he was sacked I would go back again. That's not really how it happened.

Shaun was sacked and it led to uproar amongst our supporters, understandably so being only weeks after he had led us to FA Trophy glory. One or two of the more hot-headed seemed to believe they could get Shaun reinstated. It was never going to happen relations were beyond repair.

Although I had now left the club I perversely got involved in the appointment of his successor, Mike Marsh. In communication with Rod I twice visited Mike's house in Aughton and established he was keen to take over. Me being involved must have had Frank wondering what the hell is going on. There was a feeling we had to act fast before we were lynched by supporters. Shaun had called us buffoons and I feel sure many agreed with him.

After I resigned I encouraged John Moorcroft to step into my place on the board. John seemed to have become very distant with me, clearly I had upset him in some way but not long after he had replaced me I was hearing he had moved into my seat next to Frank while making critical remarks about me.

After giving so much to the club during my eleven years as secretary I was just not having that from someone whose contribution had been a mere fraction of mine and sent in a letter retracting my resignation as a director. Despite some opposition the vote to reinstate me was carried. Things would never be the same again!

My return had nothing to do with Shaun having been sacked.

So back at the club with no specific role to fill I was pretty aimless at times. My final two years with Burscough were not that enjoyable and I don't have very good memories of them.

'THE ONE CONSTANT'

Of course we expected criticism when the next shareholder's meeting came up. I seem to recall Dave McIlwain took the chair. Dave didn't perhaps have the same baggage as the rest of us and had, for want of a better phrase, a 'user friendly' demeanour that had a calming effect. There were always those you could never satisfy however.

John Yates was a respected journalist who lived in Burscough and supported the club all his life. However, he did seemingly enjoy finding a reason to criticise those that ran the club even through those years of success that other clubs would have given their proverbial right arm for. I found it quite tiresome at times. There were those that suggested the club was a closed shop. All I can say is that I was football nobody who was accepted into the club and went on to play as big a part as anyone during my years at Burscough. The same opportunity had been there for those that were so ready to find fault.

The truth was that the one constant throughout those years were those that ran the club and the success we consistently achieved on gates that far too often failed to reach 200 was almost beyond comprehension so I didn't always take kindly to criticism.

Mike Marsh, the former Liverpool midfielder, was without doubt a high profile appointment as manager that placated at least some of our supporters. Mike appointed as his assistant Ian Bishop the former West Ham United and Manchester City midfielder whose colourful life included being a great friend of heavy metal group Iron Maiden's founder and bassist Steve Harris. Bish now coaches in Florida.

Mike's time at the club was frustrating, being beset with injuries and coming into an unsettled atmosphere to put it mildly. He went on to prove himself at the very highest level of the game going on to be first team coach at Liverpool under Kenny Dalglish and Brendan Rodgers. However, things didn't work out at Burscough and after thirteen games Mike resigned and was replaced by Derek Goulding.

Derek came over as quiet and unassuming but he was very much his own man, not so much stubborn as determined. He would listen carefully to what was said but then come back with a considered reply. He was a superb coach who had been youth team manager and played a big part in developing some of the many talented youngsters that made it through to the first team. It made sense to offer him the position of first team manager, well head coach actually, he was never going to accept a caretaker role. If anyone was going to settle things down it would be Derek and after I left he would lead the club to a sensational FA Cup win captured on Match of the Day.

Inevitably I suppose, some, but by no means all, of the FA Trophy heroes had moved on during all this tumult. One of the more surprising developments in many ways was seeing keeper Matt Taylor go on to make a league career as a central defender mainly with Exeter City and Charlton Athletic. We were aware he played in that position for Winstanley College and knew Matt was a fine all round sportsman though I'm not sure anyone saw that coming.

When Derek took over we were bottom of the league, five points adrift. One game during Mike Marsh's short spell in charge worth recalling was at home to Southport now in the same league when kick-off had to be put back with long queues still in Mart Lane awaiting admission. The attendance was 1,246 and I claim some credit for that having got Southport secretary Ken Hilton to agree to play at Victoria Park on the August Bank Holiday Monday in return for us playing New Years Day at Haig Avenue.

'A DISGUSTING PERSON'

The season was memorable for reaching the third round proper of the FA Youth Cup for the first time, not without one or two incidents along the way! A visit to Bradford City in the first round led to a stunning winning goal in extra-time from Karl Ledsham to complete a 3-2 victory, it must have been from fully thirty five yards. I recall former England international defender Colin Todd sat right behind us at Valley Parade, he was then the first team manager, and hearing him asking his assistant about Burscough. He could not have failed to be impressed, it was an incredible win by the Burscough youngsters.

I learned a harsh lesson about dealing with the press in the next round at Lye Town in the West Midlands, the winners would be at home to Preston North End. The game attracted tremendous attention down that way because in the Burscough squad was Graham Rooney a younger brother of Wayne. Although a youth game Lye had their biggest attendance in over twenty years with more than 300 present because of the publicity generated. Young Rooney was on the bench and photographers were regularly popping out to get a picture of him.

After the game and hospitality in their clubhouse we were heading back to the coach when I noticed Graham had a half finished pint in his hand. I told him to take the glass back. The next day I got a call from a guy who worked for the Non-League Paper asking about Rooney. I told him about the game, the large crowd, the result and how Rooney came to join us. I also casually mentioned about the glass. Big mistake the cretin made that the headline. I found out later he used to work for The Sun!

We won that game and went on to face Preston North End and by then we knew the winners would be away to Arsenal! This led to another story worth relating.

With only about twenty minutes played our central defender Sean Nightingale was sent off. Sean was furious and was wagging his finger and pointing at the ref. It left us with a massive disadvantage although we only lost 1-0, even striking a post in the final minutes.

We were stunned when the match official's report came through accusing Sean of having physically assaulted him. That was an incredible accusation to have made against the young lad and the potential repercussions didn't bear thinking about.

What he didn't know was that at that time Preston videoed all their games. I contacted Preston with a hope and a prayer that the video showed the incident. The guy there was most helpful and sent me a video copy of the whole game. I got my brother Brian to make a copy of the incident on a loop to be used in evidence. It clearly showed Sean never touched the referee!

I went to Liverpool County FA headquarters for the hearing with Keith Maguire who was by then secretary and would represent the club. I remember that referee arriving, cocky little sod, and thinking what a disgusting person to lie the way he had. Keith told me he backed down so quickly once he knew we had the video he nearly disappeared up his own arse. I still recall that ref's name and why he was never charged for making such a serious false accusation I will never understand.

I had enjoyed success when I made a request to the council that the road past the ground be named Bobby Langton Way but my suggestion that the sign on entering the village be changed to 'Burscough - FA Trophy Winners 2003' fell on deaf ears!

Ron Moran's grandson Ian Johnson had a spell at Burscough. Now Ron really was a Liverpool legend. He was left back when I started watching them as a kid in the 1950s. From his first team debut in 1952 until his retirement he gave the club 48 years and filled every role imaginable.

While Ian was playing Ron was a regular at home games and though he was invited to go in the boardroom he preferred to be left alone in the stand and allowed to quietly watch the game. We quickly came to respect his wishes.

One of my biggest embarrassments while at Burscough was getting sucked into what turned out to be nothing more than a publicity stunt to sign Stan Collymore who was then retired. It was in the bar at an away game that Chris Lloyd told me had a financial backer to sign Collymore for Burscough and that the player's agent had said they were interested. I was initially enthusiastic and it made some headlines but because of the controversy surrounding him and his reported vicious attack on his then girlfriend Ulrika Jonsson it didn't do the club any favours at all to be associated with this man.

I think this was really brought home to us when Gary Wright threatened to withdraw the whole junior section from the club if we went ahead with the signing. Gary was right of course and thankfully nothing came of it.

'BOMBSHELL'

2003-04 season ended in bizarre fashion and the most amazing phone call I ever received while at the club. A major reorganisation of non-league football was taking place with the formation of a Conference North and a Conference South as feeders to the National Conference.

The complex arrangements meant that the Northern Premier League clubs that finished in the top thirteen that season would be promoted to Conference North while there would be a play-off for a fourteenth club to be promoted involving the clubs finishing in the seven places below plus the Division One champions.

Having recovered from that dreadful start to the season finishing in 19th place meant we were one of the eight in the play-offs and despite playing our first two games away from home reached the final where we would face Bradford Park Avenue at their Horsfall Stadium. One problem that arose was that key defender Steve McNulty was due to fly off on holiday to Turkey that night. Extraordinary arrangements were put in place to allow McNulty to play with a motor cycle 'taxi' ready to speed him to Leeds-Bradford Airport as soon as the game finished. Unfortunately the game went into extra-time so we had the quite unforgettable sight of Steve racing from the field, now fully in holiday mode, once the ninety minutes were up.

We ended up losing 2-0 and I remember being so disappointed yet curious that one or two on the coach home appeared not to share my disappointment.

The story of this season was far from over when Telford United went into liquidation and resigned from the Conference. This led to another place in Conference North becoming available. The powers that be decided it should go to Ashton United who had finished 14th in the league. We felt strongly that once the season went into the play-offs league position ceased to take precedence and we as runners-up in those play-off should be promoted. We appealed.

All this nonsense had been taking up time. The Conference were due to have their AGM down on the south coast with nothing still sorted.

The evening before their AGM I was just getting out of my car to take my dog, Meg, for a walk on Winifred Lane playing fields in Aughton when my mobile rang. It was John Moules, chief executive of the Conference. He was literally pleading with me to get Burscough to withdraw their appeal because of the chaos it would bring to their AGM with nothing being able to be finalised. He could sense my reservations so then unleashed this bombshell. Burscough had already withdrawn their application for promotion weeks before!!!

I asked him if it was done in writing. He told me it was done over the phone. I asked him who made the phone call. He either didn't know or wouldn't say. I asked him that having withdrawn our application why were we allowed to enter the play-offs. I can't remember his answer to that one. I was so staggered by all this I'm not sure Meg even got her walk.

Following that phone call I must have phoned Frank and it was agreed we would withdraw our appeal. I remember the relief and effusive thanks from John Moules.

I was totally confused. If we had withdrawn our application why did someone at the club allow us to enter the play-offs and have supporters travel to Bradford for the final? Why did we go to so much trouble to have McNulty play? Why did we appeal?

By far my most overriding concern was the secrecy and deviousness of it, done behind my back and the backs of others. We all deserved better and it did have repercussions!

And if you think we were handed a raw deal that season just wait until next season!

We had a testimonial for Ryan Bowen in May who had given such tremendous service to the club. The turnout of former players was phenomenal and it was good to see Shaun come back for that. Some of those players like Ryan Lowe, Lee McEvilly and Robbie Talbot were registered as full-time professionals with other clubs so looking back now it horrifies me to think what the repercussions might have been if one of them had got seriously injured. Best not even go there!

'MY BIGGEST MISTAKE IN FOOTBALL'

Chris Lloyd owned the Malthouse Business Centre in Ormskirk and Neil 'Puskas' Leatherbarrow had known him well for many years mainly through local football. Neil indicated to us that Chris was interested in coming on board at Burscough.

There is no doubt we had reached the stage where new investment was needed if the club were to maintain the giddy heights we had reached, income from gates, advertising, sponsorship and fundraising alone would not be enough. At a meeting with Chris he gave the impression he could bring new money into the club, one name he mentioned was Chris Higham who owned a car dealership in Ormskirk. Nothing came of that although a guy called Andy McGregor did join u and put a four figure sum into the club, hardly a game changer but he did seem genuine and he put his staff at our disposal to design a new website. He was the owner of BT Local Business also located at Malthouse.

Whatever, in 2004 Chris Lloyd became chairman of Burscough Football Club after directly requesting that Frank step down.

Here is where I have to own up that the decision to withdrawn our application for promotion to Conference North that year without my knowledge still rankled with me. It had shown a betrayal of trust and affected how my loyalties changed. I was therefore one of those that supported that change, I was one of a group that I believe was referred to as the 'Ormskirk Mafia'. With the benefit of hindsight my bigges mistake in football was to give my support to Chris Lloyd as chairman.

Chris might well have started with the best of intentions and for a couple of seasons things seemed to be going well as the club enjoyed even more success, beating Gillingham in the FA Cup and winning promotion under Liam Watson. The question has to be asked though, at what cost? The club was clearly being run into massive debt that eventually cost us ownership of the ground. Was that deliberate or not? I will leave others more close to the action at that time to answer. At heart though Chris was a businessman always looking for the next deal.

I dread to think what budget Liam Watson had!

During the time I was at the club I can only recall Chris Lloyd putting in £500 of his own money and if any of the investment he promised ever happened I must have missed it. Duped is the word that springs to mind and I blame nobody but myself.

The day I learned Chris had gained ownership of Victoria Park I was horrified. We were one of the few clubs in the north west to own our own ground outright, having purchased it from Ormskirk Council in 1951 for £400. It had required a supreme fundraising effort to pay for it. It was something we were all proud of and what made me fume most was that ownership had seemingly been transferred virtually in secret without a struggle, no meetings of shareholders, or supporters or the public were called to inform of the situation and perhaps set up an opposition campaign or fighting fund. That was the part I couldn't forgive.

After all that I don't think anything ever annoyed me more than the day Chris Lloyd put out a statement and ended with 'Chris Lloyd, Burscough FC, Owner.' My one and only thought was, the arrogance of the man! OK he had got the ground, but owner of Burscough Football Club? Do me a favour. Him or whoever else can have all the fancy bits of paper they like but the club belongs to the village, the clue is in the name.

In the care of Chris Lloyd then Martin Gilchrist it has been depressing to see what has happened to the club and its connection with the community since I left. I don't think either have ever fully appreciated that much of the antagonism directed to them is because most supporters can't stomach the idea that the control of the club and ground has fallen into private ownership where making money from that ownership will always be the priority.

Having said that we are talking about football and a football club and I am realistic enough to know there are more important things in life.

I knew both of them personally and both went on to suffer life threatening health problems that I wouldn't wish on anyone and any comments I have made are purely about their impact on the club. I wish them nothing other than a full recovery.

'MADNESS'

I had now been at the club twelve years. During the time I was at the club I worked with some great people many of who I have already mentioned.

Tom Spencer was club physio when I arrived, seemingly always smiling I got on well with Tom. Just before I left Burscough I fell down the stairs while shifting some furniture and Tom ended up with me on his treatment table! Mel Singleton was later the physio, he was another great addition to the club we got from Southport. He was so organised, always first at the ground on match days and for away trips he would get the beer from Bargain Booze and store in cool boxes so it was always ice cold on the way home. At 50p a bottle it really helped the time pass.

Puskas, well known around Ormskirk football did a great job with the reserve side admin over several seasons, a real character, a bit like Marmite you either liked him or you didn't. Roy Webster brought in money to the club mainly through selling advertising space and continues as a passionate supporter of the club if not the people who run it. Alec McGregor the groundsman, always so pleasant, who quietly went about preparing the pitch for games and rarely complained when I gave the go ahead for a reserve or youth game in adverse weather conditions. He would just give me a look! John Fletcher was managing the youth team during my final couple of years and coincidentally I bumped into him at Asda in Llangefni after I moved to Anglesey, he worked for Asda. Dave Ball and Frank Duffy worked closely with Dave Hughes and they too brought some talented youngsters to the club.

Keith Maguire followed me as secretary who I had mixed

feelings about. He reported dutifully to the directors although I wasn't always happy about his attitude towards others. I was so proud of the youth set-up we built up over many years and after I left the club the major architect of that Dave Hughes was scathing in his criticism of the lack of support he got.

Suffice to say that during my time at secretary we had a policy of bringing in young talent, putting them on contract and thereby received transfer fees totalling well into six figures. I cannot think of one young player the club have sold for a fee since while Burscough's days of being a force nationally in the FA Youth Cup were soon a distant memory.

It is painful when I look back at what has been lost. During our FA Trophy winning season we had arrived at the point where EIGHTEEN teams were playing as Burscough FC. Four at senior level, thirteen at junior level and even a vets team playing under the club's name. None of this happened by accident.

I recall one time going back to Victoria Park and there being notices everywhere warning against foul language and racial abuse, even threats to search spectators. We had been one of the friendliest clubs around yet it made Victoria Park sound like a place you would never dream of taking your kids. It was madness though it didn't surprise me one bit.

If the ending to 2003-04 season had done Burscough no favours the ending to 2004-05 season saw us the victim of daylight robbery as a result of one the craziest decisions in the history of the game.

During what would be my final season with Burscough I still have great memories of a second qualifying round FA Cup game at Skelmersdale United's new Selby Place ground. Skem chairman Frank Hughes even asked me to do a piece for their programme. It was like old times with a crowd of over 1,000 and a real derby game atmosphere. Groundsman Peter McGee always had the playing surface looking immaculate at Skem and on a sunny October afternoon a thrilling game did it justice.

With almost £4,000 prize money at stake for the winners and Burscough two divisions above their rivals Skem were bound to be fired up for this one. In fact it didn't look good to start with as the game seemed to be going in the home side's favour but Burscough fought back in the second half to win 3-2, I seem to recall David Eaton was amongst our scorers. In the fourth qualifying round Tamworth got a small measure of revenge for their Trophy Final defeat by beating us 2-1, one goal coming from a corner with both our central defenders watching helplessly from the sidelines having had treatment for injuries on the pitch.

We had enjoyed an excellent season under Derek Goulding and looked to have finished fifth thereby securing a play-off place yet having no idea of the farce that was about to ensue, a farce that would see the incompetents at Lancaster Gate cheat us out of our hard earned chance of promotion.

With nine games still to play Spennymoor United resigned from the league leading to unprecedented scenes of chaos. The NPL at two meetings made the decision to expunge Spennymoor's record which left Farsley Celtic as champions and Burscough in a play-off place. Four clubs appealed to the FA over this decision, the FA eventually making the decision that Spennymoor's record should be reinstated and three points awarded to teams for unplayed games against Spennymoor.

It meant Hyde United were now champions instead of Farsley Celtic and with Prescot Cables having two games unplayed against Spennymoor they were quite literally gift wrapped six points for sitting on their arses doing nothing meaning they overtook Burscough by one point to claim the final play-off place.

Burscough chairman Chris Lloyd and Farsley chairman Andy Firbank were both furious at this ridiculous decision and how it had affected them and appealed to the FA without success before both clubs continued the fight to the High Court in London. It made no difference.

Still smiling. Back at Victoria Park for presentation from chairman Chris Lloyd

'THE ONLY GAY IN THE VILLAGE'

2005 was to see another big change in my life. It had been twelve years since I had finished at General Motors and I had not done paid work since so the lump sum we had received on leaving had taken something of a hammering. We were living in a semi-detached house in Ormskirk and our neighbours at that time where, shall we say, a little on the intrusive side. Along with that the open farmland at the back rarely seemed to be farmed anymore, fields of barley gently blowing in the breeze that I so loved to watch were seemingly a thing of the past. To sum up we had become unsettled living there, the kids had left home, and it seemed to make sense to downsize and free up some of the capital in our house.

I remember saying to Sally if we're going to move let's not move two miles down the road let's move somewhere completely different and begin a new chapter in our lives. Sally had now retired so the world was our lobster, well something like that.

We put our house on the market. Well, we didn't actually as the estate agent phoned some friends who were specifically looking for a house on Redgate and a viewing was quickly arranged even before it was advertised. They were a nice couple who were both involved with the scouting movement in Ormskirk. They were keen as mustard to buy and a price was quickly agreed. There was one problem, we had no idea where we were going to live so we could not commit to the sale at that time.

I spent many hours on the internet looking at property in different areas. We even went up to the Scottish Borders looking at property around Kelso, Selkirk and Melrose. A lovely area but the property wasn't an awful lot cheaper then there were the complications of selling in England while buying in Scotland where the sealed bid system they then operated was hardly compatible.

We looked around mainland Wales. I recall one bungalow on the banks of a river, it looked very nice although we were told it had been underpinned so that and the proximity to the river meant that was a no-goer. It was in a village near Tregaron called Llanddewi Brefi made famous in the TV series Little Britain. It was where Dafydd, the only gay in the village, lived. We also viewed a house in a village called Llanrhaeadre-ym-Mochnant, I actually learned how to say that years later because of the football.

The couple still had their hearts set on buying our house and that was to be tested even further as sadly we then had to have our much loved Sheltie Meg put to sleep and that upset us both so much we put everything on hold and cleared off to Crete on holiday.

We set about a house search in earnest after we returned and Sally took a shine to Anglesey, not a place we really knew well. We were struggling to find something we liked though in the price range we had set. The estate agent pointed out a new bungalow in a village called Bethel emphasising it was very much in a Welsh speaking area. That wasn't a problem then and has never been since. I had already seen the bungalow on the internet and it appeared too small but we said we would take a look. I let Sally get out of the car when we arrived and she looked through the windows. She was clearly impressed with the size of the rooms so we rang the estate agent and she came out with the key. From the moment we walked in we knew it was the one.

When we got home I left Sally to negotiate and a price was quickly agreed. It meant we had bought a brand new two bedroom detached bungalow on Anglesey for less than two thirds of the price we got for a three bedroom semi-detached house in Ormskirk, freeing up almost £70,000 in capital! After paying off the mortgage outstanding I was back to putting on my investing hat.

The couple who had waited so patiently were delighted to finally get the go ahead for the sale to go through.

We never saw the bungalow again until the day we moved in, Friday 19th August 2005.

'A HELL OF A STANDARD'

Before we moved I had looked at an Ordnance Survey map of the area and had noticed the name Glantraeth in open farmland between our village of Bethel and Malltraeth on the Cefn Estuary. I had heard of a Glantraeth Football Club, in fact I think I had one of their programmes. It seemed an unlikely place for a football ground. Well, there was and it was about a mile from our new home, I'm sure Sally thought I planned it that way!

Whatever, my final two years at Burscough had been traumatic at times and not really enjoyable so I was determined to take a break before even considering getting involved in the game again.

As soon as we moved in I went to the next home game at Glantraeth. They were playing in the Cymru Alliance which is the second tier only one below the Welsh Premier League, a hell of a standard for an Anglesey village club. The ground with a small stand was idyllically situated in beautiful countryside with marvellous views of Snowdonia as a backcloth to the game. It was clear that Glantraeth were a strong side and that would be well proven as the season progressed.

I also visited other grounds as I began to learn about football in this part of Wales. One that particularly attracted my attention was Bethesda Athletic about a twenty minute drive away on the mainland. They had a neat ground that looked ripe for development. I usually stood by the dugout and a couple of times got talking to their manager Steve. They had enjoyed some good times including entering the FA Cup and and FA Trophy, in fact the last game they played in the Trophy was against Tamworth a name of course I knew well.

I soon became a regular at Glantraeth home games, slowly becoming familiar with the player's names. Nicknames in Wales were soon to fascinate me. Whereas at Burscough it had been Blas, Clanny, Jocky, Clarky, etc, here they were far more exotic. I soon learned Darren Jones was Chicken, Richard Owen was Pigeon and best of all Mark Thomas was Cabbage. The line-up sounded more like the ingredients for a casserole than a football team.

I was soon shouting for the team and I'm sure the regulars began wondering who this strange Englishman was that had suddenly appeared on the touchline. Most had a first language of Welsh but I noticed several of the players seemed to be predominantly English speaking, many being from Bangor.

The manager of Glantraeth at that time was Paul Whelan. Paul had quite a pedigree with Bangor City having played and scored for them at Wembley in the 1984 FA Trophy Final against Northwich Victoria. A year later he had also played in Europe against Atletico Madrid including the away tie in their iconic Vicente Calderon Stadium.

As the season went on it became clear this team was in with a great chance of winning the league. One of the guys in the dugout I heard called 'Gary' was the team physio I mostly heard speaking in Welsh. I learned later he was also the chairman. Close to the ground was the Glantraeth Restaurant where you could go for a pint at half-time or after the game, it was an excellent facility. A guy I knew as Jeff did a matchday programme which considering the crowds were only in double figures was a real labour of love, often as much as fifty pages including adverts. Later I offered to do a piece for the programme about my time at Burscough which was likely the first time I alerted the club I might be future committee material.

One big game for Glantraeth that season was at home to Rhyl in the Welsh Cup, a game that attracted a record 500 crowd on a day of strong winds and heavy rain. Playing with the wind Glantraeth went two up only to have Gareth Owen sent off. Playing against the elements in the second half with only ten men the game was eventually lost 5-2.

I wasn't at that game I was 100 miles away having been an invited guest for Burscough's FA Cup game at home to Gillingham. It was good to be back at Victoria Park, things still seemed to be going well and it was nice to relax before the game with a meal and a glass of wine in the Barons. The highlights of a thrilling game were shown on Match of the Day as Burscough scored twice with time just about up to win 3-2.

'SOON IN AWE OF THIS VILLAGE CLUB'

The end of season completed an incredible introduction to Glantraeth as I slowly got sucked in. The team had a midweek game away to main rivals Buckley Town. I was invited to travel on the coach. A win would mean Glantraeth were champions of the Cymru Alliance, a win for Buckley would see them champions. A vociferous 700 strong crowd at Globe Way were there to meet us, the home support hugely outnumbering the Glantraeth contingent. Glantraeth had many players who had played at a higher level with Bangor City and it showed as they coped with the hostile atmosphere without real problem to run out 3-2 winners and secure the title. With the club also winning the League Cup they remain the only Anglesey club to complete the double at that level and I joined in the celebrations after the game, in the local conservative club I think it was.

Although the ground was never going to be good enough for promotion that was some tremendous team and over the years I got to know several of them well, particularly Gareth Owen and Warren Gibbs.

We were invited to the end of season presentation night in the Glantraeth Restaurant. We still didn't know anyone that well so I said to Sally let's just go along for an hour or two to show our faces. We were placed on one of the top tables with some of the island's biggest landowners. In the bar later over a few drinks many new friendships were made.

It was after two in the morning when we left!

I was still in no rush to get closely involved I was quite content to be just a supporter and enjoyed going to games. It was brilliant to have such a good standard of football on my doorstep in such pleasant surroundings.

I had already decided that if I was to get involved with another football club it would only be with one where I felt I could use my experience to make a difference. I believed I had identified where I could help to make a difference at Glantraeth!

The ground at Glantraeth might have been idyllically situated but I have to be honest and say it was an absolute mess in so many ways. It was difficult to conceive it was considered of a standard to host games in the second tier of Welsh football. The pitch was more weeds than grass and often didn't seem to be cut short enough, the lines around the pitch were so deep the ball would sometimes run along them rather than going

Cymru Alliance League & Cup double

out, I guess through the regular use of creosote or similar. The stand had seats, some cracked or broken, that looked like they were never intended for exterior use and was an unsightly mass of weeds beneath. The pitch side railings were too low, rusty and had boards attached that had become warped badly with the weather so just looked an eyesore. The walk from the changing rooms to the pitch was across loose weed strewn slate and gravel and a potential ankle twister for players. Worst of all there was no barrier to farm animals going into the spectator areas which in winter became a lethal combination of mud and sheep shit. That was probably what most drew the criticism of visiting spectators.

I look at the ground today and my part in the changes that have taken place as one of the achievements I am most proud of during the whole of my time in football.

I cannot remember the exact time I joined the committee although I would guess sometime during 2007. It was always going to be Glantraeth, they were my local club and I was gradually getting to know the people around the club like Gwilym Jones who was then the match day secretary. I remember Gwilym inviting me and Sally to a Welsh night in the Glantraeth Restaurant where we met his wife Olwen and enjoyed a meal then entertainment provided by a male voice choir from Menai Bridge. It was a memorable evening and we amazingly recognised Mrs Jones in the restaurant who was formerly one of the kid's teachers at Christ Church School in Aughton! She was originally from Beaumaris.

Jeff Scott who did the programme was the only Englishman on the committee at that time. He lived in Holyhead but was from Hull and a fanatical Hull City supporter.

Whatever criticism I may have made about the ground I was soon in awe of this village club. Firstly for what they had achieved on the pitch, just winning the Cymru Alliance, then learning they had knocked Bangor City out of the Welsh Cup a couple of years earlier at Farrar Road becoming the first Anglesey club in 42 years to reach the quarter-finals. Then there was the fundraising, they were just incredible. Gareth Evans the chairman was running a car boot every Sunday at Mona in the centre of the island that had been built from almost nothing in the 1980s. Every Sunday summer and winter he was up at an unearthly hour and out of the house to raise funds for the club.

His wife Helen was also the driving force behind a club lottery that generated £500 of prize money every two weeks, this in a village with a population of only about 400! It's not difficult to imagine how many tickets had to be sold to make that profitable for the club.

Of all the people I have met since moving to Anglesey I consider Helen and Gareth my most valued friends. So highly did I regard them that since the day I joined the club I consistently said if Gareth and Helen packed up so would I. They are the very heart of the club.

It was clear there was not much I could offer on the playing side the club were already successful although I like to think I have played a part in what we may have achieved since.

Playing in the Cymru Alliance meant quite a great deal of travel, many of the away journeys far more scenic than the travelling up and down motorways that was often the case with Burscough.

Our longest away journey in the league was to Penrhyncoch down near Aberystwyth travelling through some of Snowdonia's finest scenery. On one occasion we had ordered an executive coach but what turned up was one of the standard buses used around Anglesey, the driver explaining the coach had broken down. I recall us stopping at Rhostrehwfa to pick up Gwilym Jones. He took one look and had to be persuaded to come aboard. By the time we had picked everyone up there wasn't an empty seat. Even worse the seats rose in stages with the players towering over us committee members sat at the front. Players like Chicken and Cabbage were not the quietest so I recall getting a couple of bottles of beer for the journey home more as an anaesthetic than anything. It took an age, we must have stopped at every lay-by for the players to have a pee, I remember christening it the 42 bus with the outside toilet!

'GREAT MERRIMENT AT MY EXPENSE'

When I went with chairman Gareth Evans to my first meeting with the committee of the Anglesey Agricutural Society who owned Mona Showground where the weekly car boot sale was held I was staggered to learn how much rent we were paying them. It had already become unsustainable leading to us being in debt to them. The heyday of car boots was in the 1990s and by now much of the novelty had worn off, there was more competition from internet sales and crowds were nothing like as big.

Although I was new to all this I told them there was no point us carrying on the car boot as the small profit we were making was out of all proportion to what we were paying in rent.

John 'Polis' Owen was the secretary when I joined the club coming up to 25 years service. John was originally from Aberdaron on the Llyn Peninsular and had been the village policeman for many years, hence the nickname, and very much respected in the Bodorgan community. As secretary and treasurer he had kept a ledger recording all our dealings regarding the car boots over the years.

Rightly or wrongly I decided if we were going to get the weekly rent reduced we needed to take an open and honest approach so I typed out a summary from the ledger showing outgoings versus incomings to show how our profits had dropped. At the next meeting I attended again with Gareth I passed around copies of this summary. I also had with me John's ledger that I told their treasurer he was welcome to view to check any figures while making it plain we would not leave it with them.

The truth was Gareth had been managing the car boot for years and they dare not risk getting anyone new in without his knowledge and experience.

The upshot of all this was they agreed to drastically reduce the weekly rent and we were able to pay off the arrears.

It was a pleasing outcome.

Paul Whelan was manager for four seasons at Glantraeth and the club never finished outside the top half of the table, including once finishing runners-up and once winning the league. I never got to know Paul really well as I had not yet taken a prominent role in the club. His record alone at such a high level makes him the club's most successful manager. In 2008 he departed Glantraeth to take charge at Porthmadog which was to lead to a period of uncertainty for the club.

Before the end of 2007-08 season Iolo Owen decided to close the Glantraeth Restaurant, his intention was to have it converted into residential units. It was a big blow to the club as league rules stipulated we had to provide match day hospitality for visiting players and officials as well as spectators. It is true to say the timing caused some bad feelings.

A compromise was reached that we could have access to the bar area until the season ended, laying on our own food and drink.

That left us with the problem of providing an alternative. I located a portakabin fitted out as a canteen on eBay that seemed to fit the bill and we went ahead with purchasing that. The only problem was it was located in Middlesbrough so delivery cost almost as much as the cabin.

I arranged to meet the low loader with the cabin after it came off the A55 and was stood waiting for ages only to go to the ground and find it had already been lowered into place! That caused great merriment at my expense.

Helen would be the canteen manager so I came up with the brilliant idea of calling it 'Hel's Kitchen' and if Gordon Ramsay thinks he has an exclusive on that well he can &#%!ing well &#%! off.

The cabin was secondhand with a limited life, it did us for a few years before being replaced with a far superior metal cabin. The lads fitted it out as a canteen and made a superb job of it.

Later on I collected team photos covering many seasons while researching the club's history and framed and hung some of them on the cabin walls. I remember Les saying how much better it looked. It's always nice to get a word of appreciation.

With the restaurant now closed we needed somewhere for after match hospitality. At the time there were only two pubs in Malltraeth, the Royal Oak and the Joiners Arms. The Royal Oak was too small plus they were more rugby orientated and I doubt mere footballers would have been welcome. So the Joiners Arms it was. Most clubs in the league we knew got free food at their local pubs especially in a town were there was competition for business. With little in the way of competition we had to pay for food but the Joiners has proved to be what we needed and we've had some good times there.

'I GOT SOMETHING IN THE REGION OF £50,000'

Before Paul Whelan departed Glantraeth had not been a club that changed managers often but 2008-09 season was to prove an exception. Former Bodedern manager Kev Hughes started the season in charge and looked to have a strong squad that would do well yet early season results didn't augur well as there were no wins in the opening four games followed by two successive humiliating 6-1 home defeats that led to Kev being replaced by Gareth Roberts from Tal-y-bont and many of the former Bodedern players leaving.

I liked Kev and although he had been a player with Glantraeth bringing in a manager and players whose hearts were really with another island club at Bodedern was perhaps not the best of ideas. A good tactician Gareth Roberts did his best to steady the ship but was faced with a downbeat environment within the club and gave us notice before an away trip to Flint that he would be finishing after the game. In the clubhouse at Flint we had a discussion with the senior players and Emyr Rowlands agreed to take charge for the remainder of the season. We just about did enough to avoid relegation, finishing next to bottom.

Despite such a disappointing season the presentation night in the Joiners Arms was one of the best with a great turnout. Midfielder Chris Evans turned up dressed as a nun believing it was fancy dress, not that he cared either way. A great lad everyone at the club were distraught when they heard of his tragic death while still in his twenties.

I took over from John Owen as secretary in 2009. John's health was not now so good so I believe he was more than happy to pass on responsibility, I recall his son Darren telling me of the family's relief. It was around this time when I gave a presentation in the village school to the rest of the committee proposing a five year plan to improve the ground. It included increasing the hard standing to around approx 75% of the ground including the canteen area, fencing off the ground from surrounding farmland, new perimeter railings, flush toilets for spectators, new tip up seats in stand plus bricking up and providing steps at front so the stand had the look of having a solid foundation with the wild undergrowth below hidden. Although the wider tip-up seats would reduce capacity from 72 to 63 the improvement would be well worth it.

Eventually all of this was done including tarmacking from the changing rooms to the ground entrance. My main contribution was in obtaining grants from Welsh Ground Improvements. I would guess I got something in the region of £50,000 over the years, possibly more. I even got £1,000 from the phone company O2 towards outer fencing after explaining farm animals getting on the pitch were proving a health hazard.

I believed strongly that making the grant application look as professional as possible went a long way to achieving a successful outcome. I used to buy a presentation display book with clear display pockets inside for inserting documents. I included pictures of how the ground looked now and pictures generated on computer of how the ground would look following the spending of the grant money. I feel certain this was a major reason we never had one grant application rejected.

When Jeff Scott left the club I remained the only non-Welsh speaking member of the committee. I have always been appreciative of meetings being held in English to accommodate me though I did go to night school in an attempt to learn Welsh but like many English people got so far then gave up. It is difficult, although perhaps that is just an excuse. Although I can get by with the basic pleasantries I always describe my Welsh as more effluent than fluent!

It was never quite as high pressure at Glantraeth as at Burscough. Many of the committee lived in Malltraeth and had known each other since they were kids so there was no politics and no big egos. I always believed from the moment we moved to Anglesey that it was our job to fit in and not to expect others to change to accommodate us and I believe I have always been true to that.

'LOW POINT IN THE CLUB'S HISTORY'

During the 2009 close season the club was having great difficulty attracting a manager and putting a new squad of players together and with the season getting ever closer it was clear it wasn't going to happen. We had no alternative other than to resign from the league and give ourselves time to regroup and go again after a season out of football. It was a low point in the club's history.

A small village club such as Glantraeth being successful and seemingly cash rich did inevitably attract a fair amount of jealousy on the island, many of the comments uninformed and quite insulting especially on social media. It never bothered Gareth he would just make a counting money gesture to wind them up even further. The truth was that the club worked tremendously hard for every penny it earned by getting off their arses doing it rather than sitting at computer keyboards doing fuck all of any use.

Just as at Burscough I used to love going down to the ground during the week and enjoying the idyllic location, sitting quietly with perhaps just the sound of a sheepdog barking in the distance. Landowner Iolo Owen had allowed the club to play football on his land since 1984 for just a £1 per year peppercorn rent. His bungalow overlooked the ground and he would often come across to watch the games. Many a time I visited Iolo at home to discuss football issues and the view he had was just incredible. He had allowed us to do so much to develop the ground into the superb facility it now is but there would always be limits. I doubt he would ever have allowed us to erect floodlights for example, the pylons would have been too intrusive, but I couldn't help thinking it would look magnificent at night lit up in such a rural setting. Think the baseball pitch in Field Of Dreams! Build it and they will come.

One bonus of the ground being so close to home was that Sally would often walk down the lane with our two dogs, Lucy and Summer, and meet me towards the end of the game I would then run them home before heading off to the Joiners for an after-match pint.

Many of the committee like vice-chairman Les Thomas worked in and around farming and it used to amaze me how they came together when a job needed doing, particularly in the close season. They also had access to all kinds of machinery that would suddenly appear to make holes for posts then hammer the posts into the ground. There seemed nothing they couldn't turn their hands to. To a city kid like me it was all fascinating.

Les was the joker in the pack, too often at his worst when encouraged by Helen. I remember him once telling me Iolo said 'Stan is very intelligent.' I don't think he was joking but you never really knew with Les. Iolo once asked me to give him regular updates on the electricity readings on the ground saying he didn't trust those two buggers, meaning Les and Gari! As an Englishman I took that as quite a compliment.

'GLANTRAETH IN FOUR CUP FINALS'

After a season out of football the club were determined to be well prepared for their return in 2010-11 season and to prove the point appointed the management team of Kev O'Neill and Chris Roberts in January giving them plenty of time to formulate their future plans. It would prove to be another period of stability and success for Glantraeth.

Due to resigning from the Cymru Alliance the club had to drop two divisions to the Gwynedd League in line with Welsh FA rules. The league turned out to be a three horse race with Glantraeth in fierce competition with Bro Goronwy and Beaumaris Town. A poor start to the season with three losses in the opening six games left an awful lot to make up although Bro Goronwy only finished champions by a point.

It was the cup competitions that took centre stage with two quite incredible ties then a record breaking finale to the season.

In the North Wales Coast Intermediate Cup a second round tie at Trefdraeth saw Bro Goronwy beaten 8-5 after extra-time with Gary Jones claiming a hat-trick. There was an even more incredible tie in the quarter-final away to Llandudno when Glantraeth twice came back from the dead. It is worth recalling in detail.

The visitors looked to be comfortably in control as they quickly stormed into a two goal lead, both coming from Gary Jones, but Llandudno fought back and were leading 3-2 with the game going into the 93rd minute only for Craig Evans to level and send the game into extra-time. The home side then looked to have made the tie safe as they went into a two goal lead and that's how it remained with six minutes left only for Glantraeth to stage a sensational recovery. Steve Jones jinked in from the right and his low shot found the bottom corner then Gary Jones missed a great chance to complete his hat-trick. With time just about up there was more drama as holding in the area resulted in a penalty to Glantraeth and Craig Evans made no mistake with the spot kick to make it five-all and set up a penalty shoot-out...or so we thought! This amazing game had yet one more twist as with three minutes of added time played Glantraeth won it 6-5 with the last kick as Gary Jones drove a ball in from the left, finding the net with the keeper stranded.

2011 winners of four cup finals
Keith, Gareth, Stan & Les

Almost as much as the game itself my memory of that day was most of us watching the final stages of the game through a window in the clubhouse while almost hugging a radiator, it was absolutely freezing outside.

The end of season saw Glantraeth in four cup finals including all three league cups going on to create a new chapter in the club's history by winning all four in a fourteen day period, the most prestigious, the North Wales Coast Intermediate Cup, being won after a penalty shoot-out against Beaumaris at Holyhead.

Not only that with Bro Goronwy's ground failing inspection Glantraeth were promoted to Welsh Alliance Division Two as league runners-up.

At this time I must say the club seemed to be overrun with Arsenal supporters, both the management and the committee. I struggled to understand how people born and bred on Anglesey wanted to support a team in the south of England. The chairman wasn't much better, supporting Chelsea.

One thing I was very proud of at Glantraeth was the club website I developed. I got many complimentary comments from all around North Wales and it was regularly voted one of the top three. The only thing that probably let it down was that it was not bilingual in Welsh and English, a reason Porthmadog's often got top vote.

I inherited a club website from Jeff Scott then completely revamped it so that the headline news was always prominent on the front page, a bit like a newspaper. A website to be of any use has to be topical and quickly updated with news or it is just a waste of space. Ours was just that and supplied with superb action photos from Aled Jones games were invariably reported the same day.

Unfortunately, I could not hand the website over after I retired as the website needed knowledge of HTML code to be updated and that had become somewhat obsolete in club websites with the introduction of the likes of Pitchero, etc. A great deal of information about the club was sadly lost when it closed down.

Former Daily Post sports journalist Dave Jones was always complimentary about the website. He is the most committed journalist I have ever worked with and has done more for promoting sport in this area of Wales than anyone I've known.

I also took over the match day programme when Jeff Scott left. Jeff used to do an epic programme of sometimes fifty pages. There was a charge for the programme and I used to feel for Jeff if many were left unsold after all his work, and there often were.

I decided to do it a different way with just a four page programme that was free with admission, the last thing I wanted was to see my efforts wasted. I designed the outer cover in colour and had them pre-printed for the complete season with the two inside pages printed match by match with an editorial plus squad details, league table, appearances, scorers, fixtures and results. I think it worked well enough.

'CHAMPIONS IN STYLE'

Promoted to Welsh Alliance Division Two for 2012-13 season Glantraeth took the division by storm scoring 97 goals in 22 games to finish champions in style. On top of that the league cup was also won, beating Llanberis 3-1 at Caernarfon in front of a 500 plus crowd, Anthony Hughes getting a hat-trick.

A fitting end to a thrilling season was facing Bangor City at their Nantporth Stadium in the final of the North Wales Coast Challenge Cup, the Welsh Premier League Club eventually coming out on top by four goals to one.

Marc 'Loggs' Evans was top scorer with 39 goals only a couple short of the club record, another of those strikers that I have been privileged to watch over the years. With two promotions and five cup wins to their names Kev and Chris had certainly justified their appointment although Kev would now step down leaving Chris in sole charge.

One thing I found more of a problem in Wales was putting seven days notice on a player of another club. It was surprising how many clubs took it as a personal insult that you were trying to sign one of their players. I don't recall having that trouble at Burscough.

Most secretaries I had a good understanding with, appreciating transfers worked both ways. The truth was if a club made it difficult for us then I was less likely to put myself out for them. Common sense really. I recall putting notice on a Bethesda player and having to go to the Welsh FA as the secretary would not sign the transfer form, not that Cardiff were much help.

A player called Dion Donohue wanted to join us from Caernarfon Town. We were playing a night game at

Caernarfon and I was getting more and more wound up as they seemed to be avoiding signing the transfer form. In the end I gave it to our chairman Gareth to deal with before I blew a gasket. I actually ended up having a very good relationship with Caernarfon secretary Geraint Jones.

Celebrating more silverware with Kev O'Neill & Gareth

Donohue signed for us, played one game, which we lost 7-0 at Holywell, then wanted to go back to Caernarfon! Fair enough the lad went on to play just under 100 league games for Chesterfield and Portsmouth and the last I heard he had signed for Swindon Town.

I lost count of the times I travelled the forty miles up to Porthmadog to sign players. Gerallt Owen was their secretary and he worked in the Goat Inn at Dolbenmaen so I would often meet him there at lunch time, get the form signed and enjoy a half of lager. Gerallt was also one of the good guys.

Accusations of illegal approaches seemed to be an obsession with some clubs. I used to tell our managers every club does i just don't leave any fingerprints! On an island like Anglesey players and managers of different clubs socialise and work together so some of the accusations were simply ridiculous, some maybe not so!

With Bangor University being so close and having over 10,000 students I guess it was inevitable that occasionally we had players who were studying there. That could cause problems as they mostly went home at holiday times. We had a keeper Marc Newbould whose home was in Kent yet travelled up one Christmas holiday by train to play for us when we were stuck. We of course paid his train fare. We had another keeper Kyle Williams whose party trick was to turn his feet front to back through 180 degrees. Honest. It perhaps explained why his kicking wasn't the best! One student who played for us, Liam West, now lives in Melbourne and was appointed team doctor to Australia's 2020 Under 20s World Athletics Championships squad.

'AN ENGLISH FLAG BEHIND THE GOAL'

I recall arranging for Marine to come up to Glantraeth for a pre-season friendly. The Crosby club were then managed by Alvin McDonald who had not long been in charge of the Vauxhall Motors side that went to London and knocked Queens Park Rangers out the FA Cup. I think the game was a little bit of an education to the lads at Glantraeth. Unfortunately because of holidays we only had twelve players available whereas Marine brought up a squad of over twenty. Their officials arrived in their club blazers and ties and were visibly astounded by the stunning location of our ground, cameras clicking away. We held them quite well for forty-five minutes being two down and having missed a penalty but when they brought on virtually an entirely fresh set of players after the break it was all too much and they ran out 8-0 winners.

While planning a print version of this book Marine made national news after they were drawn at home to Premier League leaders Tottenham Hotspur in the third round of the FA Cup.

Another occasion I brought an English side to Glantraeth pre-season was the visit of Atherton Collieries from the North West Counties League. They brought quite a few supporters who wrote later on various blogs what a wonderful day they had enjoyed. No admission charge, cold lager, beautiful sunshine, spectacular scenery, they even won a half-time penalty shoot out against some local lads, no wonder they were so happy. The game ended in a goalless draw. What I remember most is Gareth going near apoplectic as they began to string up an English flag behind the goal!

One of the long standing committee members was Len Jones. From the day I arrived Len was always very welcoming. Sally really liked Len, I think she said he reminded her of my dad. My biggest problem with Len was he talked so fast I wasn't always sure if he was talking in Welsh or English and I was forever saying 'yer what.'

Len was the deacon of Sardis Chapel in Malltraeth and I recall going along one Sunday to get a flavour of a Welsh chapel. I chose well as the kids from Sunday school were having a presentation so there was a good turnout of parents as well. Unfortunately that wasn't typical as chapel numbers have generally fallen and not long afterwards the chapel was closed and has now been converted into luxury holiday apartments.

It was interesting to see Len in a different light at chapel where he spoke quietly to the congregation. He was very vocal at games, the match officials often getting an earful. I attended Len's funeral in Bethel when there wasn't an empty seat in the large chapel.

Our ground was in the Bodorgan area of Anglesey and for three years while he was a search and rescue helicopter pilot stationed at RAF Valley Prince William and his then girlfriend Kate Middleton lived in a farmhouse in Bodorgan, on the estate of our club president Sir George Meyrick in fact. Kate often used to visit our village shop here in Bethel accompanied by her female minder.

I wrote to Kensington Palace with a cheeky request that Kate become a vice-president of the club. I got a reply that it would be considered but she eventually opted to give her support to the Beaver Scouts on the island. Can't really argue with that.

In 2012-13 we were drawn away to Presteigne St Andrews in a qualifying round of the Welsh Cup. It was a 300 mile round trip, a quite ludicrous journey for a qualifying round although the rules were changed so this couldn't happen a couple of years later.

Whatever, it was an enjoyable day even though we ended up losing against a team that should have been well beaten. Like many of the mid-Wales clubs their facilities were excellent and they were a real friendly group of people. Presteigne was right on the English border, almost in the Wye Valley, and we didn't hear many Welsh accents. I remember most that their ground stank, it was right next to a sewage treatment plant.

Llanidloes were another mid-Wales side we visited in the national cup. It was October yet a steaming hot day. I recall standing under a tree for shade and Helen basking in her shorts. Again the facilities were superb with a bar under the stand and a good crowd of about 400. We had stopped on the way down for a pre-booked lunch at a pub in the village of Carno, most famous for the original Laura Ashley factory and another 'factory' that at one time reputably produced 50% of the world's LSD! Again we lost, 4-3, after being 3-1 up at the break.

I sometimes announced the teams over the PA system. That could be quite testing for me as an Englishman and not just some of the player's names. Prior to going to Llanidloes we had drawn mid-Wales side Pontrhydfendigaid at home. I practiced that one for days leading up to the game! We won that one 9-0, Chops, Andy Clarke and Paul Rowlands all scoring two each.

'THEY REALLY DID A HATCHET JOB ON HIM'

Ian 'Chops' Pleming was a striker who enjoyed a couple of spells with Glantraeth. On his day he could put the fear of God into any defence, he was that powerful. It was never dull with Chops around. I often used to say to Gareth we should have been trained as social workers the stuff we got involved with over the years.

Bryn Terfel, the famous Welsh opera singer, was separated from his wife and Ian was later in a relationship with Mrs Terfel which attracted the attention of the Mail on Sunday following a supposed attack on Pleming in a night club. Helped by quotes from an unnamed 'witness' they really did a hatchet job on him. Some of the stuff the journalist Nic North wrote was disgusting like suggesting he was a bad father, writing oh so eloquently 'he has a kid.' In fact he had a lovely daughter, Chloe. Basically what he was trying to do was portray Pleming as Mrs Terfel's bit of rough after a share of any divorce settlement. On behalf of Chops and the club I wrote to the paper's editor complaining about the journalist. It was no surprise to learn that Mr North now writes for The Sun.

I also threw in a request for a donation to the club as they had used a picture of Pleming off the club website without asking permission. They sent us a cheque for £200!

One memorable occasion was the visit of Groundhop UK in August 2013. Around 300 groundhoppers descended on our ground for a Saturday evening fixture against Llanrug United. As well as from the UK some travelled from mainland Europe. It was part of an event organised with our league, the Welsh Alliance, which included visits to eleven different grounds over the three days of the Bank Holiday weekend.

We really went to town erecting a large marquee to serve food and drinks as well as selling club souvenirs. Helen was in charge of the catering arrangements and as always did a brilliant job, local treats like Welsh cakes and bara brith going down well.

Reg & myself on duty for the visit of Groundhop UK

My main job was the beer. I visited Purple Moose Brewery in Porthmadog and arranged for delivery of boxes of real ale to the Joiners Arms in Malltraeth where landlord Phil Penson would store them until the day of the game. In truth I ordered far too much and the groundhoppers ended up buying a 36 pint box at cost to take back to the University of Chester where they were staying. I believe they ended up selling it at £1 per pint!

I also gave myself the job of producing 300 programmes, something of a souvenir edition compared to my normal free-on-entry four page offering. The folding and stapling of that lot took a while!

It all went off perfectly, the groundhoppers were in awe of the ground's location, the game was a cracker, Glantraeth winning 3-2, and all our hard work was rewarded with a late night drinking session sat outside the marquee after all our visitors had departed. The official attendance was given as 308.

New signing Tom Taylor scored twice in that game, one of the best players I ever saw play for Glantraeth. An English lad of tremendous talent and commitment he suffered from type 1 diabetes and it was not unknown for Helen to supply him with a Mars Bar from the canteen during a game to keep him going if his sugar level dropped.

It came as something of a shock early in 2014 when manager Chris Roberts gave us plenty of notice he would be leaving to take over as manager of Llangefni Town at the end of the season. It was understandable, it was his home town club and I guess would fulfil one of his ambitions. They also had more potential for further progress not having the ground limitations we had. Glantraeth had given him the platform for his first job in management and Chris had done an excellent job for the club over four seasons and would be a hard act to follow.

We quickly made the decision that former player Warren Gibbs would be his replacement although I made the mistake of posting the news on the website while Chris was still in charge. Chris thought that disrespectful and I quickly removed it.

'GROUND NOW LOOKS IMMACULATE'

2014 would be the thirtieth anniversary of the club's founding. I decided to research and write a club history and spent much time in Llangefni Library going through back editions of the Anglesey Mail.

We also decided to have an anniversary dinner. Iolo Owen's son Tudur was to provide the entertainment, a well known comedian and TV presenter in Wales. The Tafarn-y-Rhos at Rhostrehwfa was the chosen venue. It was marvellous to see so many players and officials from the Anglesey League days as well as from Paul Whelan's history making team of the early 2000s.

Delivering my speech

I was due to make a speech detailing the highlights of the club's thirty years but a few days before I damaged my back carting a heavy box of beer to the kitchen sink. Sally had insisted I dump it as it was past its use-by date by quite some distance. Pete at the Royal Oak had given it to me.

I ended up bedridden and in real pain, hardly able to get to the bathroom. Come the day of the dinner I was feeling a little more mobile so with some difficulty made the dinner after all and gave my speech, condensing thirty years into five minutes!

It was a brilliant evening despite the chaotic catering, overseen by a manager who hadn't got a clue. We quite rightly got a big discount after we complained.

The book was launched at the dinner and sold well. I was really pleased with it but have never received much in the way of feedback so have never been sure if I got it right. You can only do your best.

Glantraeth history book

The National Library of Wales based in Aberystwyth sent a request for a copy for their archives which pleased me.

I do remember that night wearing a new pair of shoes that were killing me. In fact I tried to sell them as they seemed too small. It was only when I got home I found there were still cardboard inserts in them!

A great addition to the club was Merfyn Roberts, known as Tarw (Bull in English), who had previously been with Gaerwen FC. He took ground improvements to a whole new level starting with the pitch that was soon weed free and with the addition of new fencing and with regular maintenance from Tarw and groundsman Cledwyn Williams the whole ground now looks immaculate. Tarw and Gareth's son Darren were perfectionists and set high standards in everything they did. Darren was the third generation of the Evans family with the club, his grandfather Huw having been one of the founding members.

Every time I go down to the ground I can't believe the transformation. Apart from the stadiums in the two major towns, Holyhead and Llangefni, I believe it is now the best appointed football ground on Anglesey.

One serious ambition on joining Glantraeth was to win the Welsh FA Trophy to go with the English FA Trophy, it was well within our capability. I had no idea if anyone previously had been associated with winning both, I have a feeling though it could have been unique.

Sadly it never happened, the nearest coming in 2014-05 season when we reached the semi-finals only to lose to Penrhyndeudraeth at Bangor.

On the way to the semi-final we were drawn at home to Penlan a team from Swansea, that was one helluva journey for them. They were a good side but we beat them quite convincingly. They enjoyed a lengthy session in the Joiners Arms after the game. Gareth asked their manager if his lads spoke Welsh. He replied most of them had rarely attended school and weren't that good at English. Coincidentally, a couple of years after I retired I sailed to the USA on Queen Mary 2 and one of my table companions at dinner was Rob McHugh who was the GP for Penlan which he described as a rather deprived area of Swansea.

In Warren Gibbs' first season we finished third but were never going to catch runaway leaders Holywell Town who only lost one game all season. That came at Glantraeth when a late goal from James Burgess gave us a 2-1 win.

'NAOMI IS VERY EXCITED TO DO THIS'

In 2015 local landowner Sir George Meyrick retired after twenty years as president of the club. We had to consider who might succeed him. We felt it should be someone reasonably high profile with local connections. We considered a few names and I mentioned movie actress Naomi Watts who I had been told lived in Bodorgan for three years as a child and went to the local village school. It was clear from comments she had made in the past that living here with her Nain and Taid was a really happy period of her life so I felt renewing a connection with this area of Anglesey might appeal to her. I am sure the rest of our committee thought I was daft when I suggested we write to her and ask her to be president.

An Internet search revealed her manager was Jason Weinberg. I emailed him requesting that he pass on an attached letter to Naomi but after a few weeks had heard nothing back. I sent a cheeky email saying 'it would be nice if I got the courtesy of a reply to our polite request.' He could easily have taken offence but he didn't. He replied that he was sorry and could I send the letter again. I did and got a reply saying 'leave it with me' which sounded promising.

I will never forget opening an email from Jason early in the morning of Tuesday the second of February 2016 telling us: 'Naomi is very excited to do this. What are the next steps. Thank you for your patience.'

I put a small piece on our website later that morning and within twenty four hours the news had literally gone global! France, Germany, Italy, Greece, Indonesia, Australia, the internet was awash with the story. For a few days Glantraeth were almost as famous as Barcelona.

We were inundated with requests for interviews from the

press, radio and TV. Gareth handled the Welsh language requests I dealt with the rest. I recall saying in one interview 'if you don't ask, you don't get' which ended up being quoted all around the world.

Once Naomi accepted the position of president and the story broke a whole chain of people in Los Angeles were brought into the loop and I found myself dealing with some really big names in Hollywood and drawn into a world that I had only read about in the past.

My main contact ended up being Robin Baum, Naomi's publicist. She told me she was a little disappointed the story had broken before an official press release. I could only say sorry but all this was a little new to us. At first I had thought Robin was a man but she sure wasn't, she is one of Hollywood's biggest hitters representing Johnny Depp, Orlando Bloom, Ryan Gosling along with Naomi and others. We soon developed a good relationship and she ended up getting me a quote from Naomi. I sent an email thanking her and telling her after my brief fling with Hollywood I was now retiring back to anonymity. She replied: 'You are very sweet! I am glad you are happy.'

We were then given direct access to Naomi's office in New York, I took that as a sign that we could be trusted not to take advantage and since that time I have refused many requests to contact Naomi over various issues unrelated to the club.

So, we had an Oscar nominated movie star as our club president and she still is!

I was told a guy called Huw Garmon often came to our games his nephew Guto Hughes being in the side. It got mentioned to me that he had appeared in a movie about a famous Welsh poet known as Hedd Wyn. I became really interested and travelled to Sain Records near Caernarfon to buy the DVD.

Huw Garmon was actually the star of the movie playing Hedd Wyn himself and it had been nominated for an Oscar in 1993 as the Best Foreign Language Film.

Committee with manager Warren Gibbs & Cookson Cup

I found the film, watched with English subtitles, very powerful and posted on the club website our further connection with an Oscar nominated film star. Gareth later introduced me to Huw at a game, he was brilliant in the film. I became fascinated with the story of Hedd Wyn who was killed in WW1 only a few weeks before being declared the winner of the Chair at the National Eisteddfod. A couple of years back I paid a visit to Hedd Wyn's restored home at Trawsfynydd and got to see the famous Black Chair.

In April 2016 Glantraeth reached the league's Cookson Cup Final to be played at Bangor City's Nantporth Stadium against Llanberis. Fifteen minutes before kick-off an email came through from Naomi Watts in New York with a short video attachment showing her holding a placard with the words: 'Good luck to all @ Glantraeth Football Club, Go get em! Love, Naomi xx.'

We won 3-0. With Warren as manager and Gareth Owen as captain it was quite like old times!

'A PHONE CALL FROM MARTIN GILCHRIST'

Even on Anglesey I have never fully left Burscough behind. Dave Hughes visited us a couple of times and even came to a game at Glantraeth. Sally got on really well with his wife Elaine and I was shocked to the core to hear that Elaine had died suddenly while on holiday. Dave must have been devastated, she was such a nice woman.

Despite all that has happened I have never had a cross word with Chris Lloyd or Martin Gilchrist. I can recall going to St Anne's Club in Ormskirk with Sally, Martin and his wife and Dave McIlwain and his wife and spending an enjoyable evening in their company.

Chris Lloyd occasionally used to visit the Anglesey Circuit, he had a passion for rallying I think. On one occasion he called at our home, with his son Ross, and later that evening I joined him and some friends at a Chinese restaurant in Menai Bridge.

Of course this was before my full knowledge of events unfolding at Burscough were known.

Even Puskas once called on his way to Ireland. Sally gave him a full Welsh breakfast that I think filled even him! He regularly used to visit Ireland because of his interest in horse racing. He once told me you don't require a passport to enter Ireland though they sometimes ask for some form of identification. He regularly used his UniBond League pass to gain entry thereby proving it is a dam sight easier to get into another country with a UniBond pass than Accrington's ground.

In May 2013 I made a rare visit back to West Lancashire to attend Roy Baldwin's funeral. Although a sad occasion it was nice to meet up with people from the club who I had not seen for many years. I was part of the guard of honour along with Roy Webster amongst others, Roy even said I looked younger! Nice man Roy. I recall speaking with Frank and Rod, Rod did give me his explanation as to why they had to give up ownership of Victoria Park. Sally once said to me if I had still been at the club it wouldn't have happened. It was nice to have her confidence but I can't guarantee I would have made any difference although I like to think I would have put up more of a fight. Having spent so much time researching the history of the club ownership of that ground was precious to me.

I still remain the second biggest shareholder in Burscough FC Ltd! Quite ridiculous really as I have never had anything in the way of communication from the company except for the time I tried to pass the shares on to the Supporters Club. The two 'A' shares I have mean nothing as the 'owners' have the majority shareholding.

In July 2020 completely out of the blue I got a phone call from Martin Gilchrist, currently the owner of Burscough's ground. I had posted on my Facebook page a picture of the main stand at Victoria Park along with a picture of the secondhand stand from Skelmersdale United that had been shipped into the new ground while asking 'Main stand at Burscough seemingly replaced by this? Someone tell me it isn't true.' I think someone posted this on Twitter which I don't use and it must have been suggested I had been taking pictures at the new ground which seemingly motivated the phone call. I was able to tell him that it was close on two years since I last visited Burscough on my way back from the Lake District when I was shocked to walk down Mart Lane and come across what looked like a shanty town!

As in the past our conversation was affable enough with Martin making promises that I will await implementation with baited breath. He promised that a 500 seat stand will be built integral with the social club, it had been held up due to the contractors having been affected by lockdown! The present stand is only temporary. There will be covered accommodation for spectators on the Crabtree side of the ground. He said 'I want it to be a ground we will all be proud of.' He invited me to attend the official opening, I said I would consider it if all the promises were kept.

The latest news as of September 2020 is that Burscough Independent Supporters Association have instigated legal proceedings in an attempt to win back community ownership of the club and the ground.

Two months later the case went to court. The accusations of fraud were dismissed out of hand with costs of about £40,000 being awarded against the claimants. You do have to wonder about the legal advice given to recommend pursuing this claim.

Personally, I have never believed fraud was involved. Whatever you may say about Chris Lloyd I always believed him and his secretary meticulous bookkeepers. However, included in the summing up it glibly says Chris waived £150,000 owed to him by the club as if it was some kind of badge of honour which only confirms my original concerns about the club being run massively into debt leading to the loss of the ground. I am open to explanation but Chris Lloyd was chairman, he surely had a duty of care, so how the hell was the club allowed to build up that level of debt. When I left the club in 2005 our debt was barely into five figures, not brilliant, but manageable. Chris Lloyd was brought on board to bring investment into the club not run it further into debt.

Again, many questions still remain unanswered.

'GOOD OLD ARSENAL'

2016-17 saw Glantraeth win the Welsh Alliance Division One by a massive sixteen points with some of the finest football I have witnessed since moving to Anglesey. We were qualified to be promoted back to the second tier of Welsh football as the ground had passed inspection. However, we were fully aware we could not develop our privately owned ground any further so come the following April we would have failed to meet the ground criteria for a second season and been relegated no matter how high we finished. You cannot cheat players by accepting promotion and not telling them that. So having won the league so easily it was hardly surprising that most of the players left as well as the manager leaving the club in an impossible position which led to resignation from the league and a season out of football while the club recovered.

In the Joiners celebrating the latest double

It was a great shame as under manager Warren Gibbs that was a quite outstanding side that would have done well in the higher league and young Corrig McGonigle was just about the best striker I have seen since moving to Wales. That season he broke the club scoring record while still in his teens.

We also went on to again win the Cookson Cup at Nantlle Vale to complete a league and cup double. I remember Reg Bryant our match day secretary pictured with the cup after that game and looking so delighted. He was another Arsenal supporter, often making a marathon journey by coach to watch his beloved Gunners. Sadly, Reg died not many months later. I represented the club at his funeral that ended with 'Good Old Arsenal' blasting out over the speakers at Bangor Crem. You couldn't but smile.

'A GOOD TIME TO FINISH'

Despite our failure to be promoted it had been a tremendously successful season and I felt it would be a good time to finish, on a high if you like. Just as at Burscough twelve years earlier I had got to the stage where preparing for another season was not something that appealed anymore. I had been doing it on and off for 25 years and I now wanted to be free to take up other interests, travel being one of them. I had lost my wife Sally late in 2015 and I had already booked a cruise to Norway for August and went on to travel extensively over the next couple of years.

Although I helped out for a while afterwards when asked it was time to get someone in as my replacement and the club struck lucky when former player Ian Fidler agreed to come on board along with his wife Sue and they have brought a new enthusiasm to the club. I was delighted this happened so quickly, it made me feel less guilty. I feel certain the club will continue to flourish under chairman Gareth Evans. Like my chairman at Burscough Frank Parr he has that stickability which means he never gives up.

In 2019 I did come out of 'retirement' a little by getting involved in the Island Games Football Tournament that was being held on Anglesey, some of the games being at Glantraeth. One of my jobs was doing the PA and playing the anthems before kick-off. I managed not to screw it up, I had been present when there was a major cock-up at another ground, that really concentrated my mind.

I even got our president Naomi Watts to record a video of support for the Tournament, sending best wishes to all of the participating teams.

I thought we made a brilliant job at Glantraeth with Helen,

Sue and Gloria providing the after-match food that seemed to satisfy everyone from Jersey, Alderney, Orkney, Gibraltar & the Outer Hebrides who played on our ground.

The tournament was a major success both in terms of organisation and also the island's men's and women's teams getting to the finals, Helen and Gareth's 16 year old granddaughter Catrin scoring in her final. It appears that that success has now been rewarded with Ynys Môn (Anglesey) being awarded the full International Island Games at a date yet to be determined.

That's about it.

The decision I took back in 1992 to leave secure, well paid employment and then go on to faff around unpaid in football for the next twenty-five years was on the surface foolhardy yet also courageous but with the love and support of Sally, sound investment and some good life choices I got there. Sally only worked part-time so some might wonder how I did it without bankrupting us, I do sometimes wonder myself.

It has been so rewarding, leaving me with a tremendous sense of achievement. I have travelled the length and breadth of England and much of Wales with Burscough and Glantraeth plus the odd excursion into Scotland, visiting some great grounds, some not so great. I have worked with some wonderful people, made such good friends in football and have so many glorious memories of thrilling games, winning trophies and the celebrations that follow.

However, of all those glorious memories it is perhaps inevitable that for sheer scale nothing can compare to Sunday 18 May 2003 when I was part of one of the most sensational cup upsets in the history of English football. As Yeovil manager Gary Johnson said while commenting live on Sky: 'For a small village to win such a big prestigious national competition is really nothing less than miraculous.'

And screw-ups?

I've had a few, but then again, too few to mention.

THE END

Printed in Great Britain
by Amazon

10389947R00098